VEDAT AKGIRAY

GOOD FINANCE

Why We Need a New Concept of Finance

BRISTOL
UNIVERSITY
PRESS

First published in Great Britain in 2019 by

Bristol University Press
University of Bristol
1-9 Old Park Hill
Bristol
BS2 8BB
UK
t: +44 (0)117 954 5940
bup-info@bristol.ac.uk
www.bristoluniveresitypress.co.uk

North America office:
Bristol University Press
c/o The University of Chicago Press
1427 East 60th Street
Chicago, IL 60637, USA
t: +1 773 702 7700
f: +1 773 702 9756
sales@press.uchicago.edu
www.press.uchicago.edu

British Library Cataloguing in Publication Data
A catalogue record for this book is available from the British Library.

Library of Congress Cataloging-in-Publication Data
A catalog record for this book has been requested.

ISBN 978-1-5292-0000-3 (paperback)
ISBN 978-1-5292-0001-0 (ePub)
ISBN 978-1-5292-0002-7 (Mobi)
ISBN 978-1-5292-0003-4 (ePDF)

The right of Vedat Akgiray to be identified as author of this work has been asserted by him in accordance with the Copyright, Designs and Patents Act 1988.

Cover design by blu inc, Bristol
Front cover: image kindly supplied by stocksy.com/Milles
Printed and bound in Great Britain by CMP, Poole
Bristol University Press uses environmentally responsible print partners

Contents

List of Tables and Figures

Table

Figures

Preface

As an academician with a long scholarly record, and a businessman with many successes and failures, I have always believed that finance was the single most powerful locomotive of economic prosperity and social progress. The industry was already properly structured but it could be even better if only public authorities kept their hands off the profession. I loved mathematical finance and enjoyed teaching it to others – with unquestioned confidence in its benefits for society.

This was all until the year 2008, when the greatest financial crisis of all times shocked the world and also when, as an irony of fate, I was appointed to chair the securities regulator of my country. Most of my tenure of office was in highly hectic meetings of international organizations, basically discussing what was wrong with finance. In time, most of my prior beliefs about the wisdom of finance started to fade away. I realized that the global financial system was fundamentally flawed and finance, in its current state, had become more harmful than useful for society. Today, I feel the agony of seeing that not much has changed ten years after the global crisis. And the call of duty was to write this short book to provoke wiser people to think about how we can fix finance.

Many people deserve my sincere thanks for their help and support. Serhat Çevikel and Ceyhun Elgin of Boğaziçi University corrected many errors in earlier versions of the book. Serdar Çelik of the OECD and Tim Reid of Deutsche Bank provided valuable data. Paul Stevens, Caroline Astley-Brown and Ruth Wallace of Bristol University Press were graciously supportive through the whole process. Anonymous reviewers' comments were much improving. I am thankful to the Turkish government for tasking me with regulating financial markets in the midst of a global crisis – a task which turned out to be the school of a lifetime. Last but not least, I thank my wife and daughters for their patience and support. They did not read a single page of the book but they loved the pink cover, maybe signalling that it is time to put some pink into colorless finance.

ONE

A Short Story of Finance

Money is in every facet of our lives and any activity involving money is possible only through the services of the financial industry with all its markets and institutions. Finance serves the purposes of:

1. Payments system to match payers with payees;
2. Market mechanisms to match savers with businesses;
3. Financial planning for old age and wealth transfer between generations; and
4. Managing monetary risks in business and personal lives.

The basic function of finance is intermediation between people and businesses with surplus income and those who need capital for investment or consumption. Financial markets and institutions are expected to intermediate through efficient mechanisms with optimized transaction costs and proper governance. The more efficient a financial system is, the faster the turnover rate of capital will be for more production to better serve social and economic well-being. It is a platform of allocating capital to its best uses, both spatially and intertemporarily. A sketchy chart of the finance industry is given in Figure 1.1.

Figure 1.1: Picture of finance

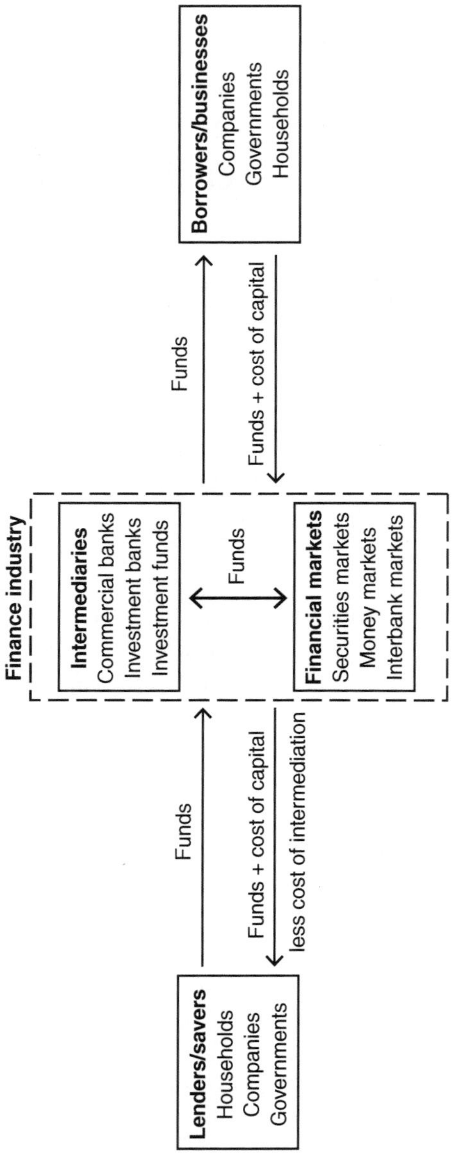

This is an oversimplistic picture of the finance industry today and the actual ecosystem has become much more complex in recent decades. From the figure, there are two takeaways from the book:

- Without a finance industry, lenders (savers) cannot match with borrowers (businesses) that need money for investment in real productive assets, a costly impediment to economic growth. Therefore, the financial industry is probably one of the most vital infrastructures of societies, maybe second in importance after energy.
- Finance is a "contingent industry" in that, without a real economy producing goods and services, there cannot be any value to its existence. Without a link to the real economy, it can exist only as a casino of bets and games played by casino owners and gamblers.

People save now to consume more later, or to have satisfactory income levels in old age. Similarly, people invest now to have a greater economic value later. The rate of profits from the real economy (where companies invest and produce) must therefore be greater than the total costs of capital and intermediation. Otherwise, businesses and borrowers would not use the available funds. People could not save through the system, or they would not lend except for charitable purposes. Companies would not need much financial management and bookkeeping accountants would suffice. In other words, real economic activity is the actual and only source of life to a sustainable financial system.

Simple reasoning and historical developments show that societies need finance for economic welfare and growth. Since the industrial revolutions in the 19th century and the technological revolutions in the 20th century, countries with more effective financial systems developed faster. The current global landscape of economic well-being evinces this historical fact. The term "effective" basically means ease of access to finance and operationally efficient intermediation. Two cases in point are given below.

Figure 1.2 shows the average number of automatic teller machines (ATMs) per 100,000 adults in high, middle and low income countries for the period 1980–2015. Although they have not been of much interest in "financial academia", ATMs have replaced many routine functions of commercial bank branches and resulted in easier transactions at much lower costs for customers. In a 2009 *Wall Street Journal* article, Paul Volcker, former chairperson of the Federal Reserve Board, characterizes ATMs as the only useful financial innovation in recent years. Indeed, the positive correlation between national income and use of ATMs can be clearly seen in the figure. The number of ATMs in high income countries is almost double that in middle income countries, and low income countries have negligible numbers of this facility. A country would need to have a developed banking system to install and operate a network of ATMs for easy access by people.

The second case in Figure 1.3 is about the size of financial markets relative to the size of an economy. For simplicity, financial market size is measured as the sum of debt and equity markets, ignoring other markets such as derivatives. Economic size is measured by gross domestic product (GDP). Total debt is

Figure 1.2: Number of ATMs per 100,000 adults

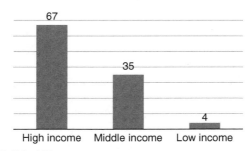

Data source: World Bank [6]

Figure 1.3: Financial market size as percentage of GDP

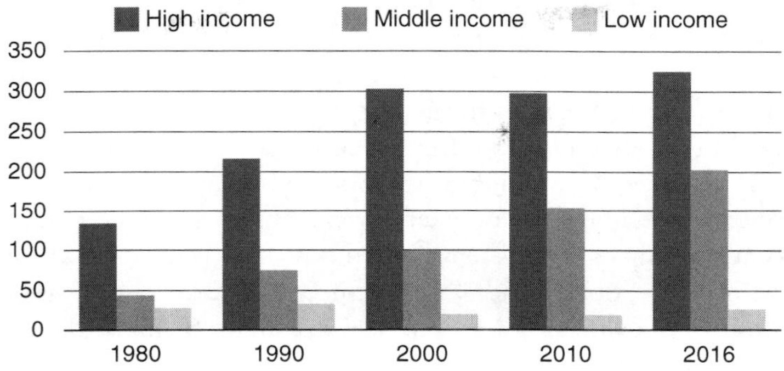

Data sources: World Bank [6] and WFE [7]

calculated as the sum of household, non-financial corporate and public debt. Size of equity markets is routinely the total market value of all listed companies in stock exchanges. It is evident that higher income countries have much larger financial markets relative to economic size than lower income countries. Since 1980, the size of financial markets has grown to more than three times of GDP in high income countries and to about double of GDP in middle-income. In low income economies, financial markets are smaller than a quarter of their national income – showing a problem of access to finance. Larger financial markets have available more debt and equity capital for businesses to tap into, and this is vital for economic growth.

As a note in passing, the narrowing gaps between high and middle income countries in recent years is largely due to the emergence of fast-growth economies such as China, India, Brazil, Russia, South Korea, Indonesia, Mexico and Turkey. These countries did not have developed financial markets in the 1980s and most of the 1990s, and they relied on capital from the developed countries to finance their growth. Hence, the fast growth in the financial markets of developed countries is due to not only increasing domestic demand but also external demand by these emerging economies. Since the late 1990s, however, financial markets in emerging economies have developed to serve domestic businesses and thus the narrowing gap in the figure. Country names in the lists of "developed markets" and "emerging markets" are likely to be revised in the near future.

Both cases are presented without any claims of causality or optimality. They are only empirical observations and many other examples may be envisioned but there is no need at this point. The bottom line is that economic and social progress is almost impossible without a well-functioning financial system.

Since the 1980s, globalization of free trade transformed finance into a giant global industry with powerful multinational banks and non-financial corporations controlling the flow of capital across national borders. The industry grew both in monetary size and product sophistication, in coverage and depth unprecedented in any recorded history of economics. In retrospect, several reasons may be cited for this development. The rise of pro-market liberal politics in the advanced economies of the West with subsequent waves of deregulation and the emergence of fast-growth economies in the East, with ever increasing need for capital transfers and loans from the West, laid the foundation of this new financial world. Finance became (or was repositioned as) not only more necessary but also more profitable. Advances in computing and communication technologies were other strong enablers of advances in finance, as an academic discipline and also as a profession. The best talents from the best schools all over the world were attracted into financial institutions, often with high salaries and other lucrative incentives. In academia, teachers and researchers in finance were paid higher salaries than those in other departments, often a few times higher than their colleagues, even in fields such as engineering and medicine.

From an alternative perspective, underlying all the events promoting the finance industry were also some fundamental sociological changes brought about by the internet in the 1990s.

Information was now freely and easily available to all people around the world. Everybody knew how everybody else lived, what they wore, the houses they lived in, the cars they drove, the trips they made, how they shopped and so on. With the additional push by platform-based business models to continual search for a "better everything" in life, consumption in excess of income quickly became the global lifestyle. Consuming more than income is possible only by borrowing. And the giant finance industry now had all the tools and freedom to design credit products for almost anyone who wanted and for any income and risk profile. Consumption euphoria was satisfied and often fueled by conveniently available credit, which further pushed up consumption on more debt, and so on. Given such a self-feeding cycle of extravagance, the finance industry could only get bigger, and it did.

So, the 21st century started out with all imaginable factors in favor of the financial industry: friendly political atmosphere, powerful new technologies, geniuses working for it, and continually increasing demand for debt. Wall Street and the City now occupied a higher priority than "Main Street" in the agendas of politicians, innovative technology companies, governments and corporations in need of financial guidance, and talented new graduates looking for high-paid jobs.

On the macroeconomics front, which is inherently linked to financial markets, the turn of the century also marked a period of comfort and triumph. After the dramatic and successful campaign by Paul Volcker to raise interest rates in order to bring down the double-digit US inflation below 5% in the mid-1980s, central bankers and monetary economists were convinced the century old problem of recessions and depressions had been solved. Lower and controlled inflation would eventually drive down interest rates, which was good for business. In 2003, Nobel laureate economist Robert Lucas echoed the opinion of many by saying the "problem of depression prevention has essentially been solved". Two years later, another reputable economist, Ben Bernanke, who would soon become the Fed's chairperson, described the two decades after the mid-1980s as an era of "great moderation". Indeed, it was a period of low inflation, low interest rates, subdued financial price volatility and satisfactory economic growth. The low interest rate environment was naturally conducive to the credit boom during the same period. In all of the advanced economies, financial stability was finally achieved with minimum probability of depressions.

When the year 2006 arrived, all was good, or at least seemed so. Much of the world economy was growing, inflation was largely under control, interest rates were low, housing prices were up, asset prices were up, and liquidity and credit were abundant. On the other hand, it was also true that, since the early 1980s, there had been some episodes of financial crises in some markets and countries. In the USA, the so-called "savings and loans crisis" from 1986 to 1995 resulted in the collapse of more than a thousand savings and loan (S&L) associations, which had given out long-term fixed-rate loans using variable-rate short-term funds. When interest rates increased, they simply went bust. The interesting end of this story is that the S&L problem has been swept under the rug through a number of bailout schemes and changes in accounting rules. No prudential or regulatory resolution mechanism was effectively implemented. The stock market crash in 1987 and the junk bond crash in 1989-1990 triggered by the collapse of Drexel Burnham Lambert, one of the largest bond traders, were followed by the debt crisis in Mexico in 1994, which later spilled over to Argentina and Brazil.

The Latin American crisis was almost replicated in Southeast Asia in 1997-1998, affecting most of the countries in the region including Malaysia and South Korea. Then came the credit default event in Russia in 1998, which took down Long Term Capital Management, the famous hedge fund run by a group of Nobel laureates in economics. One year later, in 1999-2000, the dotcom bubble showed once again how irrational markets may behave and how destructive financial euphoria can be when financed by easy debt. In 2001, Turkey went through a costly banking crisis with dozens of banks becoming insolvent, an event very similar to the S&L crisis in the US only a decade before. Most of these events were limited in scope within a small number of countries or markets. With help from the International Monetary Fund (IMF), and in some cases the US government, they were contained without significant contagion to other countries and markets. (In this context, help largely means new credit to finance realized or expected losses.) Nonetheless, signs of trouble from markets did not stop. Bear Stearns in the US and Northern Rock in the UK were about to throw in the towel. Defaults on mortgage debt had started to emerge – many big banks were reporting losses on mortgage products – but sales of new mortgage-based home credit packages continued without much interruption.

A small minority of economists struggled to warn that it was all too good to be true but their voices were mostly unheard amid the loud music of financial euphoria. The mood in major financial centers around the globe then is best described in the words of the CEO of Citicorp in 2007: "as long as the music is playing, you've got to get up and dance". The music had already stopped but the chaotic noise of the dancing crowd must have been confused for music. Defaults on home credits, triggering foreclosures and fire sales, were driving down home prices. But then, in the spring of 2007, the Fed's chairman Ben Bernanke and many other policy makers still believed that the growing number of mortgage defaults was not a reason for concern. The IMF's 2007 Financial Stability Report drew a rosy picture of the global economy.

All but a few continued to dance until September 15, 2008, when the collapse of Lehman Brothers, a century-old investment bank run by a team of financial math geniuses, made global headlines. The whole world was shocked and all the dance noise came to a sudden stop. It was the calendar date of the greatest financial crisis of all times, if not the greatest recession.

And if it were not for the unprecedented bailout package of the US government to prevent a chain crash, the global financial system was very likely to collapse rapidly. The system seems to have been "saved" (whatever that may mean) but the crisis then spread to other parts of the world, first to Europe and then to other regions. The global financial system's imminent collapse may have been prevented but the real cost of the crisis was huge. In the US alone, total loss in American people's wealth due to declines in home and equity values was more than $13 trillion. Financial losses aside, the human cost of the meltdown was also tremendous. Millions of people lost their jobs and homes, pension savings were wiped out and the social trauma was painful. In some ways, the 2008 crisis was worse than the 1929 Great Depression. Stock markets fell by 58%, house prices by 18% and household wealth by 15% from their most recent peak values in 2008. These numbers were 43%, 6% and 6%, respectively, during the Great Depression.

With a little imagination, the social and political changes the world has been going through in the 10 years since (rise of populism, re-emergence of nation-state ideologies, recent political choices in North America and Europe, Brexit, East-West trade wars and so on) may all be related to the great financial crisis of 2008 in one way or another. It is beyond the scope of this book but historians, sociologists and political scientists will certainly have a lot to say on this. Time can be a remedy for material losses but people's trust in the competence and fairness of governments and financial institutions may be gone for a long time to come. And finance without trust is a dangerous game. It seems that the crisis is not over yet and the finale is anybody's guess.

The global financial crisis of 2008 did not happen because of any economic problems previously known to central bankers and monetary economists. To the contrary, we were all made to believe in the fairy tale called the "great moderation" and that we would live happily ever after. Nor did it happen because of war, major political conflicts, or a great natural catastrophe. It happened for no good reason at all. It was new and different. It is as if Charles Dickens, in *A Tale of Two Cities*, wrote the following words to tell the story of finance over the last 40 years:

> It was the best of times, it was the worst of times, it was the age of wisdom, it was the age of foolishness, it was the epoch of belief, it was the epoch of incredulity, it was the season of Light, it was the season of Darkness, it was the spring of hope, it was the winter of despair.

The world of finance since the 1980s has been incomparably different from any time in its history. Figure 1.4 shows the number of financial crises per year since 1600 and the cumulative number of crises.[1] The total number of crises from 1600 to the mid-1700s is less than 3 and the number until 1980 is 31. This number jumps up to 66 crisis events from 1980 to 2017. In other words, the number of financial crises during the last 40 years is greater than that during the previous 400 years, a remarkable increase in frequency.[2] It is also striking to note that, after the Great Depression in 1929 and up until 1980, there was no major crisis event (except for inflation problems due to the oil embargo in the 1970s, a non-finance event) in developed Western countries, which enjoyed tremendous advances in economic welfare during the same period, especially after the Second World War. Baby boomers seem to have lived "the best of times" and "the age of wisdom" when they started out with their careers in the 1960s and 1970s. Clearly, since the 1980s, the financial industry seems to have entered into a new realm of facts.

If history carries any lessons for the future, there is much to be learned from the past few decades of financial crises. As damaging as it may have been socially, the best thing that may have come out of the 2008 global financial crisis was (hopefully) the realization of the systemic interconnectedness of world

Figure 1.4: History of financial crises

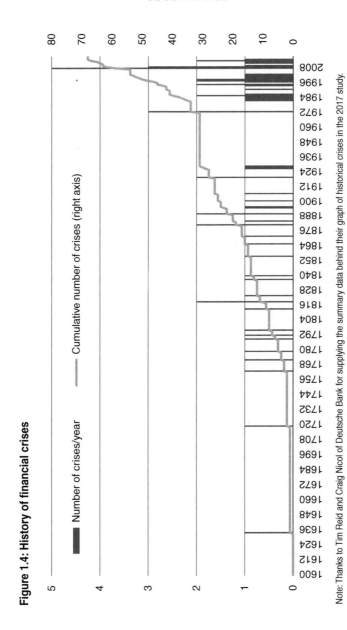

Number of crises/year
Cumulative number of crises (right axis)

Note: Thanks to Tim Reid and Craig Nicol of Deutsche Bank for supplying the summary data behind their graph of historical crises in the 2017 study.
Data sources: Reid et al (2017) and author's calculations

markets and how a flawed financial architecture can be globally destructive. Just like we need good food for good health, we need finance for socioeconomic wellness. But eating "too much good food", or taking any amount of "bad food", will damage our health. This is analogous with having too much finance, or the bad type of finance, hurting society. Indeed, all of the financial crises, small or large, during the new age of technology since the 1980s can be linked to the size of finance and its inner problematic models. Real reasons triggering crises may be political, social, psychological or technological events but crises would not be so deep and damaging if finance did not pour gas on an initially small fire to make it much bigger.

As a case in point, one of the root causes of the global financial crisis of 2008 is often and correctly claimed to be the political desire to expand home ownership in the US and in the UK. It is a fact that political decisions may be and often are populist and underestimate unintended consequences. But could the political will to expand home ownership have turned into a subprime mortgage meltdown if the financial industry had not designed and provided complex mortgage-based instruments to hide real risks? The answer is a definite no! How could an estimated total loss of about only $500 billion on bad mortgages threaten a global banking system with assets in excess of $100 trillion? Small flames were turned into a global fire by financial engineering. The whole financial ecosystem is flawed.

There are major problems with finance, both as an industry and as an academic discipline. The size of the industry is too big relative to the size of the real economy. There is excessive dependence on debt and debt-linked contracts as opposed to equity financing. The intermediation process has turned into a black box due to unnecessary complexity of markets, instruments and regulation. There are also the twin problems of the financial profession posing as unique and special on one hand, and central bankers being perceived as the only power of economic policy on the other hand. Despite all that happened during the last few decades, and even after the global crisis in 2008, the state of finance has not changed to provide any sense of comfort and confidence. There is a deep intellectual resistance to self-criticism and change. This is unfortunate and the doors are wide open for worse events at any time. Therefore, without any further delay, we need a public discussion to redefine the role of finance in our lives and to emphasize its function of serving the whole society as its foremost responsibility. Finance is not about finance only.

TWO

Problems with Finance

If an economy is characterized as a coin, then one side of the coin is the real sector (with all its tangible and intangible real assets) and the other side is the financial sector. If the fundamental function of financial markets is the translation of household savings into real business investments, then the aggregate value of financial claims must be equal to that of real assets.[3] Given this ground-zero description, historical evolution of financial markets is best portrayed alongside the developments in the real economy. And this has much to do with intense global economic integration over the last 50 years.

Size of the industry

Historically, the first era of globalization, with its peak in mid-1800s, was largely in the form of powerful imperial countries trading with less developed regions rich in natural resources. This era came to an end during the First World War. The years between the two world wars of the past century was a period of high geopolitical uncertainty and hence very low international trade and investment. After the wounds of the Second World War were mended, however, economic globalization, with great help from technological advances, significantly improved people's standard of living all over the world. Globalization has been criticized – often correctly – for many shortcomings and social challenges, such as deterioration in income distribution and domestic political instabilities. But the fact of the matter is that trade liberalization, which is both a by-product and also an enabler of economic globalization, has been materially beneficial for most countries and people. Figure 2.1 shows world's total GDP and also GDP per capita since 1960.

World GDP has increased from less than $1.5 trillion in 1960 to about $11 trillion in 1980. Since then, it has jumped up to $81 trillion in 2017. This is a remarkable added value of almost $70 trillion in less than 30 years. More importantly for economic wellbeing, GDP per capita has increased to $10,700 in 2017 from a dismal $450 per person in 1960, which is equivalent in purchasing power to only $1,280 in 2017. This could not have been possible without global economic integration and free trade. GDP, by itself, may not be a proper measure of human happiness – especially above a certain threshold and when higher income is not fairly enjoyed by all – but it is certainly a measure of income to spend. It is the way out of poverty and

Figure 2.1: World GDP and GDP per capita

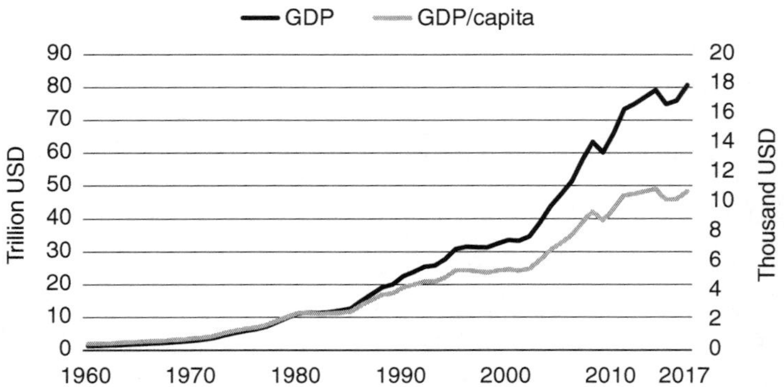

Data source: World Bank [6]

into prosperity. This has indeed been the case for many poorer countries in the 1960s and 1970s.

From one perspective, two direct enhancers of growth in a country's GDP are domestic demand for consumption (a term economists like better is "domestic absorption capacity") and foreign demand for the country's goods and services. Between 1960 and 2017, the ratio of domestic consumption to GDP has remained almost constant within a narrow band of 58–60% worldwide. Consequently, the remarkable increase in the world's GDP during this period is further explained by the growth in cross-border foreign trade.

Total foreign trade is defined as the simple sum of exports and imports of a country. The ratio of this sum to GDP is in turn called "trade openness" and, as a first-step measure, it shows how capable and open a country is to trade with other countries. In the absence of unfair regulations and trade agreements asymmetrically favoring one side, free trade is always beneficial to all involved because comparative advantages can be shared. This is because free trade comes with options of "do not buy – produce" or "do not produce – buy". The actual world of trade is of course more complex, with many layers of detail, but, mathematically, a trading space without constraints cannot be smaller than one with constraints. Free trade under fair conditions is globally good.

Back in 1960, when world's total GDP was $1.5 trillion, global trade was about $300 billion, implying a trade openness of 23%. Since then, GDP has grown almost 60 times while world trade has increased 144 times, reaching $45 trillion in 2017, and trade openness has doubled to 55% of GDP. This is a phenomenal expansion in global trading activity.

It may be useful to decompose and analyze the trends in global trade into two groups as advanced (developed) and emerging (growth) economies.[4] The countries in these groups make up about 90% of world GDP, 80% of world trade, and they have been the global game makers over the past half-century. The growth in global trade can be easily explained by factors related to the economic, financial and technological developments in these countries. To name a few, increasing consumption demand in all, increasing demand by emerging economies for new technologies (including financial arrangements) of advanced economies, increasing demand by advanced economies for the natural resources of emerging economies, and the migration of economic power from the West to the East are some of these factors.

As shown in Figure 2.2, between 1970 and 2017 the total GDP of advanced economies has grown from $2.2 to $43.1 trillion, a cumulative annual growth rate of 6%. In the emerging economies, the growth has been 9% per year, from $360 billion in 1970 to $27.4 trillion in 2017. The growth in trade has been at annual rates of 8% in the advanced economies and 12% in the emerging economies. As a result, trade openness has increased from 17% to 48% and from 24% to 47% of GDP, in the emerging and developed markets, respectively. All countries have grown fast but emerging countries have grown faster and emerging countries started the game with less developed financial infrastructures. This is probably one of the factors behind financial globalization to be discussed below.

As a side note, the growth in global trade seems to have stalled after the financial crisis of 2008 and hence trade openness has declined. This is more visible in the emerging world and it may be related to the deleveraging in the global banks of the advanced economies since the crisis and subsequent cuts in bank credits to emerging markets. However, this is unlikely to be the start of a downward trend in global trade because the finance industry has no shortage of tools to design new debt. Indeed, at the time of writing this book, several new reports show a big increase in corporate bond issues and non-bank credit to replace lower supply of bank credit. If debt, be it bank credit or bonds or any other type, is available, global trade's long-term direction can only be up.

Figure 2.2: World trade openness

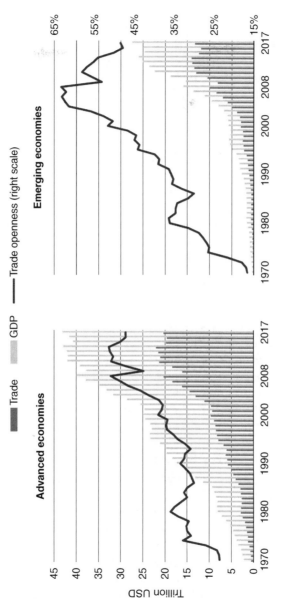

Data source: World Bank [6]

In today's world, international trade cannot take place without an underlying financial system. In the simplest setup, it would require an international payments mechanism in different currencies and an institutional network to ascertain the timely matching of payments and deliveries (that is, clearing and settlement). These in turn necessitate convertibility and exchange of currencies, bank guarantees such as letters of credit, and operational links between banks in different jurisdictions. Further proliferation of trade across different countries and industries then calls for financial instruments to manage risks related to currency values, optimization of production and logistics facilities, sustainable access to raw materials, coping with different regulatory and tax codes in different countries, and finally geopolitical foresight. The result has been horizontal and vertical integration of the global value chain and this in turn has given rise to giant multinational corporations and financial institutions.

The reflection of such an intense global economic integration in finance has been an unprecedented increase in the volume of financial flows between countries. These flows include foreign direct investments (FDI), portfolio equity and debt investments, and direct credit flows between institutions in different countries. For a given country, these flows are either inflows ("financial liability" for the receiving country) or outflows ("financial asset" for the sending country). Several organizations such as the World Bank, Organisation for Economic Co-operation and Development (OECD) and Bank for International Settlements (BIS) keep track of and report these financial asset and liability flows. The sum of such cross-border financial assets and liabilities, both inward and outward, measures the size of international finance. Similar to the concept of trade openness, the ratio of this sum to GDP is called "financial openness". Figure 2.3 illustrates the growth of global finance in comparison to global trade and income since 1980. (Th_e numbers prior to 1980 are so small that they would be invisible in the scales of the graph and they are not reported.)

Figure 2.3: International finance and trade

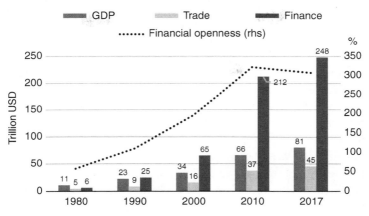

Data source: World Bank [6]

The growth in global finance has been many times bigger than the already phenomenal increase in the world's GDP and global trade from 1980 to date. Today, global financial activity is more than three times GDP and more than five times total trade. Financial openness has increased from about 50% in 1980 to more than 300% in 2017. This development needs a good explanation. And these numbers do not include any derivatives trading such as currency swaps, interest rate swaps, and commodity futures trading, and they only include debt and equity flows. If all these were also included, financial openness could easily jump up to 2,000% or even higher. To add further to the puzzle, FDI flows have ranged between 1% and 8% of GDP, with a median value of less than 3% per year. So the rise of multinational non-financial corporations and global value chains alone cannot account for this phenomenal growth in finance. It must then have to do with global banking and, to a lesser extent, the recent consolidation trend in stock exchanges.

It seems that the growth in finance has had little to do with the growth in global trade and direct foreign investments in real assets. Global banks and financial traders must have been buying from and selling to each other financial contracts of all sorts, which often have little or no relevance to the real economy.[5] This is further evinced in Figure 2.4, where the ratio of financial openness to trade openness is shown separately for advanced and emerging economies. The widening gap between financial and trade openness is largely stemming from the advanced economies, where the ratio has increased from less than twice in 1980 to more than nine times in 2017. The same number is under three times in 2017 in emerging countries, and the average ratio for the world is less than six. Before the 1970s, this ratio was always less than two and often around parity.

When data is studied more closely, five countries with large economies stand out as leaders of global financial openness. These are the UK, USA, Japan and Germany from the advanced group and, since the 1990s, China from the emerging group of countries. Figure 2.5 summarizes these cases. The United Kingdom represents the most extreme case, followed by Germany and the USA. If the trend seen over the past couple of decades continues, China will be a contender in the not

Figure 2.4: Ratio of financial openness to trade openness

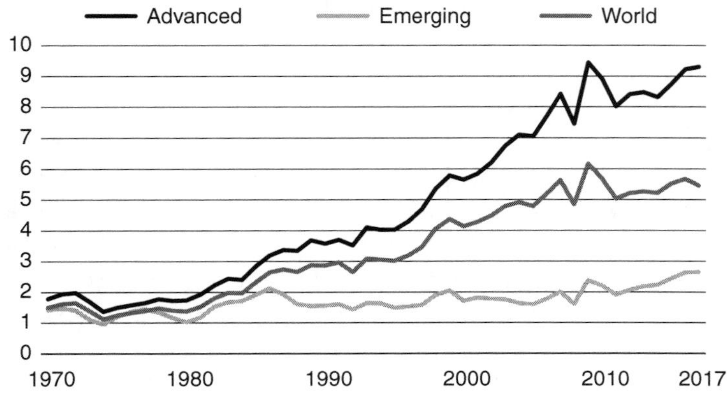

Data sources: World Bank [6], BIS [1] and OECD [3]

too distant future. Countries such as Switzerland, Belgium, Netherlands, Singapore, Luxembourg, Hong Kong, Panama and Ireland (sometimes referred to as "financial centers") also have very high financial openness levels but their GDP levels are much smaller than these five countries. As details are informative here, the numbers behind Figure 2.5 are presented in Table 2.1.

As of 2017, the UK has the highest financial openness of about 12 times GDP, and Japan has the second place with a ratio close to five. Traditionally, the Bank of England does not hold many

Figure 2.5: Leaders in financial openness

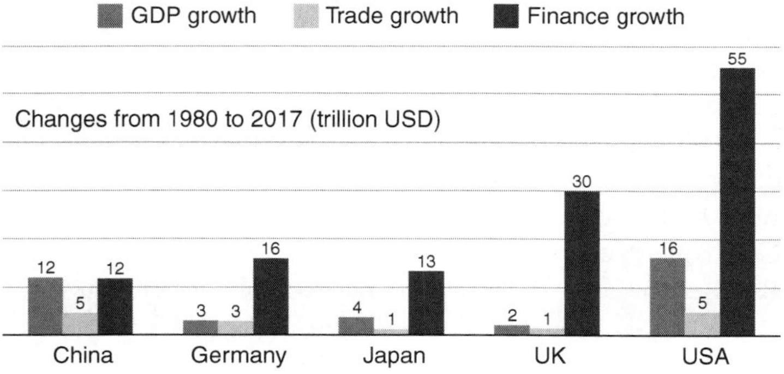

Data sources: World Bank [6], BIS [1] and OECD [3]

Table 2.1 Leaders of financial openness

	GDP		Trade		Finance		NFA	
	1981	2017	1981	2107	1981	2017	1981	2017
China	289	12.238	29	4.626	25	11.741	12	1.676
Germany	716	3.677	354	3.196	483	16.341	37	1.581
Japan	1.202	4.872	337	1.578	407	13.680	11	2.957
UK	541	2.622	260	1.638	1.193	31.134	52	−147
USA	3.211	19.391	623	5.552	1.333	56.799	121	−8.053

Note: Numbers are in billions of USD. NFA is net financial assets (including official reserves without gold) minus financial liabilities.

reserves in foreign currencies and this is why the net financial assets (NFA) is slightly negative. The interesting point about the UK is that the total sum of financial assets and liabilities is more than $31 trillion, which is larger than Germany and Japan combined, two countries with much larger economies and much higher foreign trade. This obviously has to do with London being a global financial center. In the City, they seem to trade a huge volume of financial assets and liabilities with no direct connection to the real economy. The City is the star example of "finance for finance".[6]

The US has the highest sum of cross-border financial contracts ($57 trillion) but it is also the largest economy with a GDP of almost $20 trillion in 2017. In relative terms, the case of Wall Street is not as extreme as the City. But there is a unique catch about the US. Since more than 60% of world trade is done in US dollars and more than 70% of international financial contracts are denominated in dollars, the Federal Reserve does not need to carry high reserves in other currencies, and hence the negative NFA balance of about $8 trillion. For the exact opposite reason, all other countries' central banks have to hold sufficient reserves in US dollars and their positive NFAs are largely explained by their levels of dollar and dollar-denominated reserves.

China has been the fastest growing country with respect to GDP, foreign trade and also financial openness. Recent trends imply that China will reach much higher levels of financial openness in the near future. Volumes of international financial flows will keep increasing, not only in the developed world but also in the growing Eastern economies led by China. Problems of size are being globalized too.

Assuming no major natural or political disruption in free market economics, the world economy is forecast to double in size to more than a total GDP of $150 trillion in 2050 according to a report by PricewaterhouseCoopers (PwC) researchers. Based on the trends between 1980 and 2017, global trade volume will be more than $80 trillion and the size of global financial flows will exceed $500 trillion (again excluding derivatives trading). However, the accuracy of such long-term predictions will also depend on the changing allocation of economic power across the globe. By 2050, the GDP share of advanced economies with developed financial markets (Australia, Canada, France, Germany, Italy, Korea, Japan, Spain, UK and US) will decrease to 20% from the current 35% level, and the share of fast-growing economies (China, Brazil, India, Indonesia, Mexico, Russia and Turkey) will increase from 30% to 50%. The share of the European Union will be less than 10%. Therefore, in addition to what the advanced economies do, the future of global finance will also depend on the financial business models these growth economies will adopt as they develop their markets. It may be business as usual, or hopefully a better model.

Regarding the relation between the real economy and size of finance, it may also be useful to look at the evolution of global household wealth. The sum of financial wealth and non-financial wealth equals total global wealth. Household financial wealth is the sum of direct equity holdings, indirect equity holdings through mutual funds and private pension shares, net of their debts. Non-financial wealth is the total value of houses, other private real estate, and properties of privately owned companies. As shown in Figure 2.6, global total wealth has significantly increased from $102 dollars in 2000 to about $240 in 2017. And it seems that households have borrowed (a debt balance of about $40 trillion in 2017) either to increase their wealth or to consume more, or both.

Despite a much wealthier world, the ratio of gross financial wealth with debt to non-financial debt has always been only slightly more than unity – between 1.04 and 1.2 since 2000. So, the enormous growth in financial openness cannot be attributed to growth in non-financial wealth, just as it could not be explained by growth in trade either.

Households in North America (mostly in the US) own half of the world's financial assets, and those in Europe and Asia-Pacific

Figure 2.6: Global wealth, in trillion US dollars

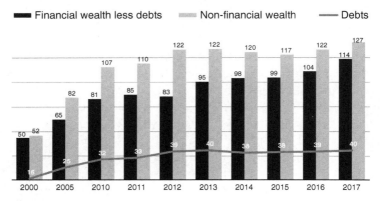

Source: Shorrocks et al (2018)

countries (including China and India) own slightly less than the other half (48%). However, Asian and European households own more than 72% of global non-financial wealth, with North Americans holding 23%. North America is "more finance", Europe and Asia are "more real estate". Wealth shares of Latin America and Africa are very small. Details for 2017 are given in Figure 2.7. Between 2000 and 2017, there have not been any major changes in the distribution of global wealth. The US has maintained its share in the world. Europe has lost some share in financial assets but gained in non-financial assets. Asia-Pacific has increased its share in both categories. Latin America and Africa have regressed in both.

Regardless of regional differences, there is also a worldwide inequality in wealth distribution, similar to the inequality in income distribution. Based on *Forbes* magazine's 2017 list of billionaires, the total wealth of the top 85 richest people in the world is roughly equal to the total wealth of the poorest half of the world. Historically, such a high degree of inequality has never been seen and financialization is likely to have had a role in this.

Figure 2.7: Geographical distribution of global wealth

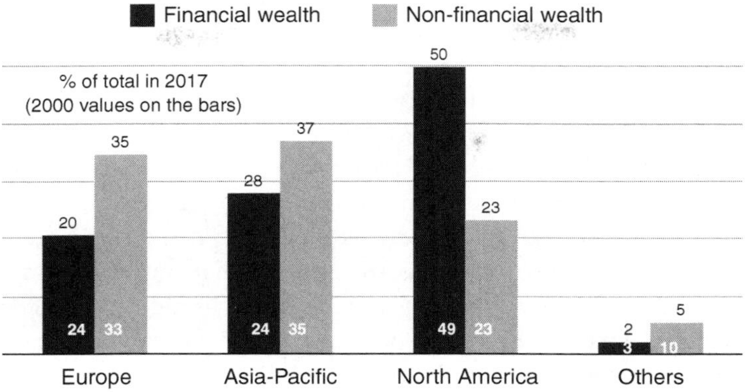

As the world's wealth and trade flows cannot fully account for the mere size of global finance, direct measurement of market sizes and values of financial assets can give further insights into this seemingly complex puzzle. There are basically three fundamental categories of financial assets: equity, debt and derivatives. Financial assets that are issued and traded in public markets – either organized securities exchanges or over-the-counter (OTC) markets – are included in the measurement of market sizes.

The size of equity markets is measured by the total market value of publicly traded shares of common stocks of corporations. The global total market value is the sum of share prices multiplied by the number of shares outstanding in all stock exchanges of the world. Although private equity is a growing market segment and off-exchange trading of private equity shares is becoming more popular, they are not considered here as part of public equity markets. In any case, the size of private equity is still very small compared to the size of public equity and inclusion would not change the overall picture and story of the book. Likewise, venture capital is also not included. Equities of privately held companies are naturally excluded because they are not tradable as securities in public markets.

It is difficult to come up with a mechanical definition of debt. Most financial obligations are properly defined as debt but some are not. Therefore, the exact amount of debt is difficult to measure because of differences between terminology and accounting methods used by different organizations and countries. Furthermore, some types of debt originate outside of the standard banking industry and regulated financial markets. In particular, non-bank credit intermediation, sometimes labeled as "shadow banking", has been declining in advanced markets since 2009 but non-bank and "non-market" types have been gaining rapid popularity in emerging markets (especially in China). And, in these countries, they are either not clearly reported at all, or reported under a variety of opaque titles in the footnotes of financial reports. Size of debt markets reported here will therefore be an understatement of actual global debt but the reported numbers are still large enough to see the big picture.

Debt is typically studied in three groups as private debt, public debt and "financial debt". Private debt is the gross debt of households and non-financial corporations. Public debt is the gross debt of governments and related state-owned enterprises. Financial debt is the net debt of banks and financial firms, largely cross-border bank-to-bank credits and short-term domestic loans between banks and other financial institutions. Private and public debt includes all debt instruments: bank credit, loans, corporate and government bonds of all types, and other financial account payables. To the extent that they are standardized, government guarantee schemes are also included in public debt. Financial debt, on the other hand, is more difficult to measure precisely, because of the presence of complex transactional flows between banks, domestically and globally. Financial debt figures reported here are largely measures of only non-derivate-based credit flows between banks, implying a positive probability of some measurement error on the downside.

Derivatives are contingent claims on financial assets such as stocks and bonds, and physical assets such as commodities. Although not a topic in the daily lives of most ordinary people, the history of derivative contracts dates back centuries and today they play a vital role in the working of financial markets. There were derivatives trading in the markets of Istanbul, Amsterdam, Paris and London in the 18th century and later, in the 19th century, in Chicago and New York. Today derivatives are widely traded in all major exchanges and OTC markets. There are derivatives written on almost any asset, or any attribute of asset values. An incomplete list includes stocks, stock market indices such as Standard & Poor's (S&P) 500, bonds, interest rates, currencies, volatility measures such as the volatility index (VIX) of the Chicago Board of Options, precious metals, agricultural commodities such as wheat, energy commodities such as oil and electricity, metals, minerals and many more, not to mention derivatives on derivatives.

There are three basic types of derivative contracts. Simple options are contractual rights (options) to buy (or sell) an underlying asset at a fixed price until or at a fixed date in the future. Forward and futures contracts are defined in the same way as options but with a fundamental difference in that they are contractual obligations (not freely exercisable rights) to buy (or sell) the underlying assets. The third type of derivatives is swap contracts, which have by far the highest volume of trading globally. A swap is a bilateral contract to exchange (swap) well-defined financial flows, often calculated on a notional principal. Finally, any combination of basic derivatives is also a derivative and the set of such combinations is limited only by human imagination.

For most people, common stocks, bonds and bank credit are easily understood and often well-known instruments, at least definitionally. But more complex types of debt such as convertible bonds and asset-backed securities are not so at all. When it comes down to derivatives, definitions and terminology are like words from outer space for ordinary people in all walks of life. That is the way they are designed to be because they could not exist otherwise! Hopefully, the meaning of this strange claim will be clear after the last page of the book is read.

Figure 2.8 illustrates the evolution of financial markets between 2000 and 2017. During the period, the total equity market capitalization grew from $27 to $80 trillion, including a $15 trillion increase in 2017 alone. The global gross market value of derivatives has increased from about $2 trillion to $16 trillion. The total market value of debt contracts (including household, corporate, government and financial debt) has gone up from less than $70 trillion in 2000 to almost $270 trillion in 2017. Adding it all up, the global total value of financial assets has shown a phenomenal growth from $98 trillion in 2000 to $363 trillion in 2017. On average, the breakdown of this total has been 75% debt, 20% equity and 5% derivatives. It is a world of debt.

Relatively low share of derivatives in the total size of financial assets (3% in 2000, peak of 10% in 2009, and about 4% in 2017) should not be misinterpreted. The notional value (the value of

Figure 2.8: Size of financial assets

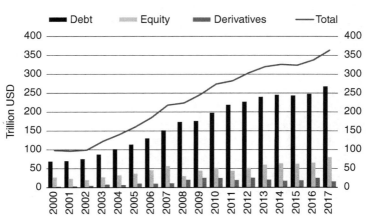

Data sources: World Bank [6], BIS [1], IMF [2] and WFE [7]

underlying assets on which contracts are written) of derivatives is a more informative indicator of the activity in derivatives markets. Notional values since 2000 are given in Figure 2.9. The total value of underlying assets controlled by derivatives has been about $700 trillion in recent years, a sevenfold increase since 2000.

Before 2000, derivatives trading was largely confined in organized exchanges and was on much smaller notional values. In December 2000, the Commodities Futures Modernization Act was signed into law in the US. The main goal of the new law was to clarify the division of responsibilities between two regulatory agencies, the Securities and Exchange Commission (SEC) and the Commodity Futures Trading Commission (CFTC), and also to regulate OTC derivatives. The purpose was largely accomplished but, as is often the case, there were also a few unintended consequences. Most importantly, doors were opened wide for trading of OTC derivatives on almost any asset and with minimal reporting requirements for supervisory oversight. The consequence was an explosion in notional values and also a variety of new – mostly destructive – derivatives such

Figure 2.9: Notional value of derivatives

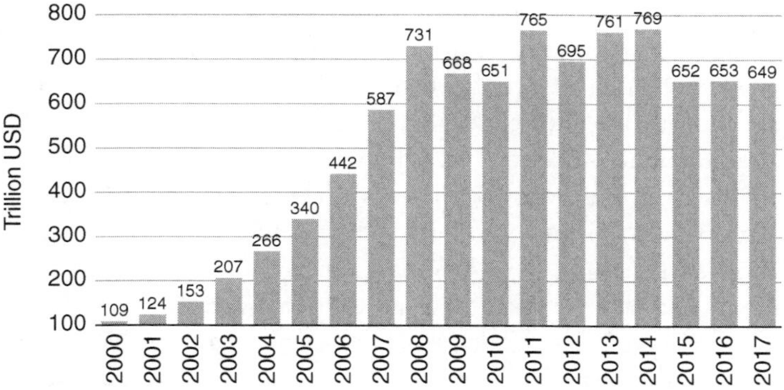

Data sources: BIS [1] and WFE [7]

as credit default swaps, which helped trigger the 2008 crisis. More on this later.

After the 2008 financial crisis, there was a global consensus on the necessity to better supervise OTC derivatives. Since 2014, first in the US and later in Europe, most OTC trading takes place via central counterparties, and trade repositories have been gathering and monitoring trading data. The slight drop in notional values after 2014 may be partly due to this new supervisory watch.

About 80% of the total notional value shown in Figure 2.9 are interest rate contracts, 10% are currency-related contracts, and the rest are commodities, equity-linked assets and credit default swaps (famously known as CDSs). Most of the derivative contracts are traded in the OTC markets (85% of total notional value) in the form of swaps and outright forwards. The remaining 15% are exchange-traded futures and options. Counterparties in derivative contracts are either dealers and financial institutions or non-financial customers. Non-financial customers are corporations using derivatives for hedging purposes, price speculators and commodities traders. Their share in total notional value was only about 20% in 2001 and has since further decreased to 10%. So the bulk of derivatives trading is apparently among financial institutions, a case of "finance for finance" with no connection to real-world needs.

All things considered, the cumulative annual growth rate in the size of finance has been 8% during the last two decades, and this is to be compared to a 5% growth in both global GDP and global non-financial wealth during the same period. Today, as shown in Figure 2.10, the ratio of finance to GDP is about 4.5 times (up from 3 in 2000) and that to global real wealth is almost 3 times (up from less than 2 in 2000). Except for a short down-and-up movement, even the global financial crisis of 2008 has not slowed down this fast growth trend to any visible degree. Neither the growth of national incomes nor that of real wealth can fully explain the current size of financial assets.

Figure 2.10: Relative size of financial assets

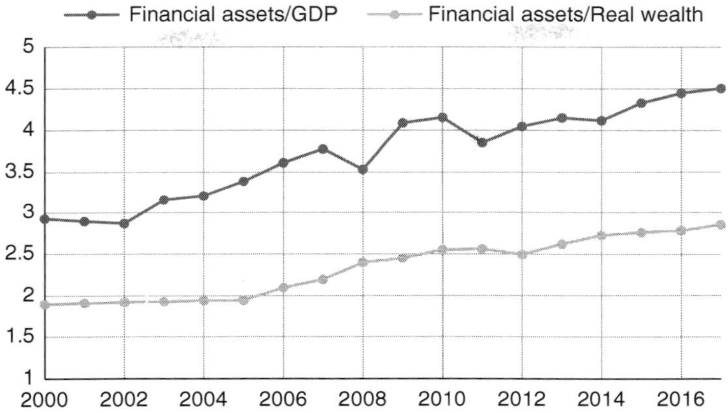

Data sources: World Bank [6] and IMF [2]

The extraordinary growth in the size of financial assets is a phenomenon of the period since the 1980s. Earlier history does not have any record of such growth. This is particularly true for bigger advanced economies such as the USA and UK. For example, Figure 2.11 shows the story of the US markets after the Second World War. Size of financial assets was less than twice GDP until the 1980s and today it is almost five times GDP. Similar pictures are to be observed in all of the advanced economies and some of the larger emerging economies. However, remembering that the US holds half of global financial wealth and that most global trade and financial flows are denominated in US dollars, the US financial industry has clearly been the locomotive of the global growth in finance.

As the enormous growth in finance cannot be adequately explained by growth in trade and wealth, there is a "black box of finance" that needs further digging into. In Chapter One, a clear positive correlation was shown to exist between economic development and size of financial markets. High income countries have larger financial markets than low income

Figure 2.11: US financial assets/GDP

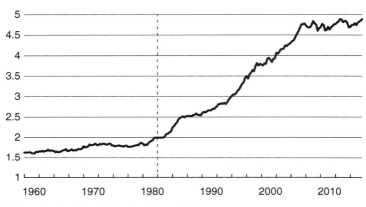

Source: https://fred.stlouisfed.org/graph/?g=smH

countries do. This is natural for two reasons. First, expanding real economic activity increases demand for financial services – business leads the growth of finance. Second, further economic expansion is possible with access to a more developed financial industry – finance leads the growth of business. Where the size of the financial markets relative to GDP is small, growth in financial services is almost certainly conducive to higher economic growth and human welfare. Societies cannot prosper without a well-functioning financial system. This is all good and true but financial crises keep pouring in, implying an inherent problem with the size of finance. Can "too much finance" be causing economic instability and market crashes?

Does more finance always contribute to higher real productivity? If so, are there size-related limits to such contribution? In search of answers, it may be useful to measure the value-added share of the finance industry ("finance income" for short) in total GDP. In simple GDP accounting, the value-added share of a sector is calculated as the difference between sales revenues and cost of goods sold. In industries with low capital intensity (as in financial companies), this difference is roughly equal to the sum of employee income (wages, salaries and bonuses) and net profit. In the finance industry for the period 1970-2015, OECD estimations show that profits on average make up about 50% of total finance income, employment (that is, size of workforce) about 30% and wages about 20%. The relative contribution of employment stopped growing in the 1990s and today most of the value-added share of finance comes from profits and wages. Bonuses are part of profits and wages.

Figure 2.12 shows the value-added share of the finance sector in GDP of the US since 1900s and the OECD countries (excluding the US) since 1970.[7] In the US, except for a spike around the Great Depression of 1929, finance income has stayed at less than 3% of GDP during the first half of the 20th century and under 4% until the 1970s. Since then, it has increased to about 8% and, except for a seemingly temporary drop after the 2008 crisis, appears to be staying at around that level.[8] The growth trend of finance income in the OECD countries has been similar. Its share in total OECD GDP has increased from 3% in early the 1970s to the 5–6% band in the 1990s and seems to have stabilized at that level. This slowdown marks a divergence from the continued upward trend in the US but

Figure 2.12: Finance income as percentage of GDP

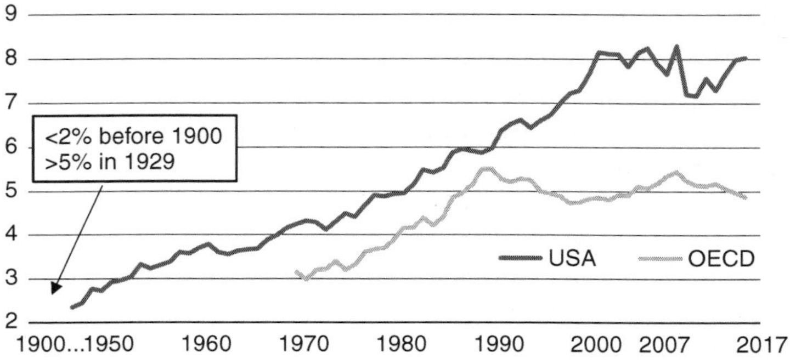

Data sources: OECD [3] and Philippon [4]

it may be a temporary divergence. This is because emerging (member) countries with less developed financial industries have been increasing their shares in total OECD GDP. Time will tell how finance evolves in these countries.

Income to the finance industry is cost to households and corporations who use the industry's services. It includes both costs of credit intermediation and also costs of asset management. In a vanilla case of credit intermediation by a traditional commercial bank, it is simply the spread between deposit and lending rates of interest. For the bank, interest on deposits is cost and interest on credit is income. In more complex cases where the intermediary is also the originator of credit, there may be a myriad of intermediaries and suppliers of funds, each naturally trying to make money from its own services. Asset managers, as the name suggests, manage the financial assets of people, corporations and sometimes governments. They constitute a huge industry of investment funds (money market funds, mutual funds, pension funds, hedge funds, sovereign wealth funds and so on) and their income is usually classified as "asset management fees".

Over the last half a century, businesses of credit intermediation and asset management have become intermingled. Now, it is like everybody in finance doing everything about finance. As the financial system gets more complex, it becomes more difficult to trace the intra-industry distribution of financial income and also the system runs the risk of becoming more costly for the society. Complexity in any facet of economics comes with its unique costs and dangers of instability. Indeed, this has been the story in finance for a long time.

Figure 2.13 shows that, in the US economy, the size of financial sector and income to the sector have grown in parallel and with almost perfect correlation. The income of the finance sector has been a fairly constant proportion of the size of the sector. Calculated differently, unit cost of intermediation as a percentage of GDP (graph on the right in Figure 2.13) has been

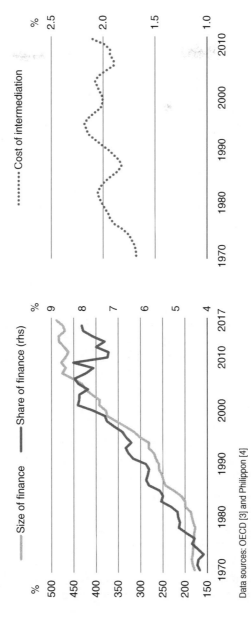

Figure 2.13: Size, share and cost of finance as percentage of US GDP

Data sources: OECD [3] and Philippon [4]

around 2% for decades. This number is also roughly equal to the ratio of finance income to size of finance. This is strange because there are no economies of scale in financial services! Why would a bank earn a larger spread on a $10 million loan than on a $1 million loan? When stock prices are rising, why would an investment bank or a stockbroker receive a higher fee from their clients? Why would it cost more to manage and advise on a given pension fund when markets are up?

Putting all this aside, rapid advances in information technologies and synergistic gains from globalization alone would be expected to yield significant decreases in unit costs of intermediation and asset management fees. In other words, the relative share of finance income in GDP should have decreased with market size. To the contrary, it has increased steadily. An inverse relation between scale and productivity is a puzzle not seen in any industry but finance. There is only one plausible explanation. The total income of the finance industry is not only higher – as it should be to make a profit – but many times higher than the true cost of financial intermediation. Using John Kay's (2015) words, this is only possible by using "other people's money". On Wall Street, in the City and in many other corners of the world, financial institutions buy and sell other people's assets, or derivatives of those assets, and make a lot of money. In textbooks, this sort of activity is not mentioned as a function of finance.

As an example of how financial activity can grow for no real reason, consider the subprime mortgage market in the US before the 2008 crisis. Subprime mortgage credit means home credit to people with low credit ratings and hence high probability of default. As bad as the idea may be, subprime loans never exceeded 10% of all mortgage credit in the US and, globally, all subprime mortgages made up only a tiny part of banking assets. So the "real thing" was small. Financial engineers, masterfully extrapolating on an old idea of mortgage securitization, then pooled these mortgages together and designed the so-called mortgage-backed securities (MBS). Different MBSs were pooled together again, now under the name of collateralized debt obligations (CDO) and traded in markets. Then, default-insurance contracts such as credit default swaps were written not only on the original mortgage credits but also on parts of all subsequent MBSs and CDOs. Not only the original lenders but also everybody else could buy CDSs on mortgage products. It was much like a long chain of speculators speculating on other speculators, who were all trying to outguess the same market with little or no regard to underlying real fundamentals. As a result, the industry built "bubbles" worth trillions and trillions of dollars of financial assets the value of which depended only on homebuyers' payments of subprime mortgages, which were worth no more than half a trillion dollars at the maximum. It was what some call "murky finance" but there were tremendous returns for financial players of the game.

Global markets enjoyed incomparably larger volumes of trading than what Humbert Wolfe (1930, 11) observed back in 1930: "In the City, they sell and buy. And nobody ever asks them why. But since it contents them to buy and sell, God forgive them, they might as well" (*The Uncelestial City*). The hormone-injected growth of finance may be interpreted as a natural outcome of free markets and hence it should not be a reason for concern. It may also be claimed that financial markets generate socially valuable information, the value of which is not considered in calculating costs of intermediation. These may all be true but no one can explain why productivity decreases with scale. There is simply too much finance.

The problem is not one of mere size but of how that size is achieved and what socioeconomic harm it may cause. Experiences of recent decades and several new empirical studies[9] have clearly shown that until there is some 'optimal' level of financial intensity more finance is good for economic growth, but beyond that level it turns bad. As mentioned before, economic growth requires a supporting financial system.

Emerging countries with small and underdeveloped financial systems, these studies show, have room to expand their financial markets to fuel their economies. At this point in history, however, they would be well advised not to allow runaway growth in finance and not to repeat the mistakes of developed economies by leaving finance in a black box. Finance should not walk faster than regulatory capacity and institutional quality. Otherwise, risky tradeoffs between growth and stability would emerge and that is not desirable.

The case is very different for developed economies such as the US, UK and most OECD countries with big and sophisticated financial industries. As the size of finance exceeds a certain level relative to the size of the economy - and it has in all developed economies – more finance slows down domestic economic growth and increases global financial fragility. There is a negative correlation between the rate of growth of finance and the rate of growth of real production. In other words, excessive finance reduces overall factor productivity. There are several reasons for this. First of all, since debt is the easiest type of financial contract to design, too much finance usually means too much credit to low-profit and high-risk projects, both domestically and internationally. This is especially easy when tax codes favor debt and regulation provides unwarranted comfort in excessive credit giving by banks, such as implicit too-big-to-fail guarantees. Excessive debt and miscalculation of underlying credit risks inevitably generates "boom-and-bust" cycles, which in turn slow down the real economy in the long run. Just remember 2008 and its aftermath.

Another mechanism through which too much finance can be damaging is the self-feeding cycle of "more volume – more pay" in the industry. The overwhelming criterion for wage premia in finance is generation of more business (more credit, more trading volume and so on), and just more business for any reason. This results in greed running in front of wisdom, and best talents being attracted into finance. Talent is needed when "real resources" are exhausted and "virtual resources" are to be engineered. Talent is needed to generate huge trading volumes out of a tiny real asset. Of course, it cannot be denied that talented workers may have a positive impact on financial technology, but when booms are busted, most of their work is wasted and the cost of waste is borne by the rest of the economy. The society would have been better off if part of this talent could be utilized in sectors with greater socially useful productivity.[10] As the saying goes, there are too many bankers and too few engineers.

Back in 1984, Nobel laurate economist James Tobin described the state of finance then:

> I confess to an uneasy Physiocratic suspicion, perhaps unbecoming in an academic, that we are throwing more and more of our resources, including the cream of our youth, into financial activities remote from the production of goods and services, into activities that generate high private rewards disproportionate to their social productivity. I suspect that the immense power of the computer is being harnessed to this "paper economy", not to do the same transactions more economically but to balloon the quantity and variety of financial exchanges. For this reason perhaps, high technology has so far yielded disappointing results in economy-wide productivity. I fear that, as Keynes saw even in his day, the advantages of the liquidity and negotiability of financial instruments come at the cost of facilitating nth-degree speculation which is short-sighted and inefficient. (Tobin, 1984, 14)

Wise people speak wise words and it seems that earlier generations were wiser in many ways. Since 1984, the financial industry has changed beyond recognition and mostly in ways Tobin was so critical about. Since then, the scope of finance has further shifted away from intermediation – the basic function of finance – and towards "non-intermediation" activities such as trading with high payoffs. As such, instead of producing economic value, financial activity extracts informational rents from the real economy. Too much finance slows down the growth in real productivity.

Textbooks teach us that financial deepening can reduce income inequality because low and middle income households will have more access to credit. Credit can be used to start up family businesses, to finance education, to smooth out lifetime consumption, and of course to buy homes. Access to credit by the poor is easier when credit conditions are more relaxed. When conditions are more constrained, the poor cannot find credit easily because they do not have sufficient collateral and credit histories. So the argument goes but neither empirical evidence nor simple logic supports it. First of all, regardless of how tight or relaxed credit conditions may be, the rich will always have easier access to credit than the poor because they have more collateral and longer credit histories. Secondly, the rich have access not only to credit but also to other financial assets such as stocks and can enjoy the returns on these investments.

When credit is expanding and stock prices are rising, it is obvious that income distribution will be distorted. Most importantly, if political populism calls for easier credit to the poor (as in the subprime mortgage credit boom leading to the 2008 crash) and regulatory laxness follows suit, the poor will naturally enjoy borrowing money, on which it is likely they will eventually default. And when defaults hit, it will again be the poor who lose more. Therefore, it is an illusion that, with the type we have today, more finance can reduce income inequality. Experience and many studies show that just the opposite is true (Cecchetti and Kharroubi, 2015; Cournède et al, 2015; Sahay et al, 2015; Lane and Milesi-Ferretti, 2017). Delivering easy credit to the poor distorts income distribution, sooner or later. The whole concept of "access to finance", which is a popular issue in the literature on poverty and income inequality, has to be redefined. More credit to those who cannot pay it back is not proper access to finance.

In fact, simple arithmetic tells us that lack of economies of scale in a sector which grows faster than the overall economy will negatively affect income distribution. It is sometimes noted that wages in finance have increased faster than other sectors' wages and, since they are high anyway, this causes more income inequality. As was shown before, it is true that finance income has increased phenomenally since the 1980s but that alone is not the problem. The real problem is that their contribution to economic productivity has not been commensurate with their income. That ends with more income inequality.

There is too much finance. But then how much is too much? What is an optimal market size for finance? An academic answer, which has no explicit practical meaning whatsoever, is that a reasonable theoretical stopping time is when a zero-sum trading activity starts to become positive-sum for financial players and negative-sum for all others. Several researchers have tried various econometric models to estimate an optimal size for financial markets in countries at varying levels of development. They are useful studies and often quite informative. However, it would be a mistake to suggest a magical formula for policy makers to decide about the size of financial assets. A wiser approach is to identify the diseases, clean them out, and then let free markets do the rest. It is always a smarter policy to regulate what should not be rather than to regulate what should be.

Too much debt

Considering that more than 75% of all financial assets is debt and more than 80% of derivatives' notional value is interest rate contracts, it is fair to say that the world of finance has become a world of debt. Too much finance, especially when debt and debt-related assets are involved, can be harmful. This picture is often termed "financialization" but a more informative wording may be "extreme indebtedness" with no apparent social good.

All agree that the one-word explanation for the crisis was debt. In 2008, global debt was almost three times that of global GDP and three times the global value of public equities. The world was clearly in "technical bankruptcy" and the subsequent crash could not be prevented. Today the situation is even worse in many ways. Debt is now more than three times global GDP and, despite bullish equity markets ever since the crisis, the ratio of debt to equity has increased further. Finance has not stopped delivering too much of its risky type.

After the 2008 crisis, national regulators and international standard-setting institutions introduced tighter controls to curb excessive credit by banks and also by non-bank intermediaries such as shadow banks, to limit non-credit activities of banks such as proprietary trading, and stronger equity cushions in bank balance sheets. References to the Volcker Rule, the Dodd-Frank Wall Street Reform Act in the US, Basel III rules and new MIFID (Markets in Financial Instruments Directive of the European Union) regulations in Europe occupied popular headlines in everyday media. For purposes of better consumer protection and of clear procedures to resolve bank failures (especially of bigger "systemically important" banks) in the future, banks were required to have more equity and lower financial assets in their balance sheets.

The term was "deleveraging" of bank balance sheets and it was successfully implemented. As shown in Figure 2.14, in Europe and most of the OECD countries, domestic credit to the private sector by banks as a percentage of GDP decreased from peaks in 2008 down to pre-crisis levels. The most dramatic drop in leverage was seen in UK banks, retreating from a high of 200% in 2008 to about 130% in 2017. The UK credit-to-GDP percentage was the highest in the world before and during the 2008 crisis, and it was still the highest in 2017. The US banks have shown the least variance and stayed in the 50–60%

Figure 2.14: Deleveraging of banks

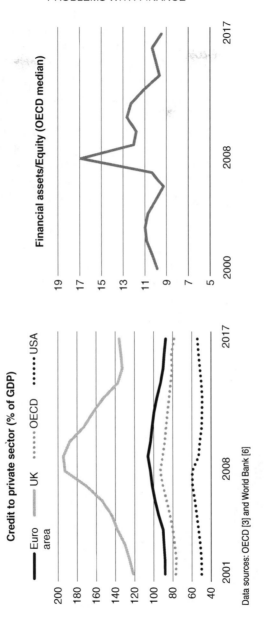

Data sources: OECD [3] and World Bank [6]

band between 2000 and 2017. Using an accounting measure of leverage, the second graph in Figure 2.14 displays the median ratio of financial assets (credit and credit-like assets) to equity of banks in the OECD countries. The ratio has peaked at around 17 in the year 2018 and subsequently declined back to pre-crisis levels of 9–10 times. There may be differences among countries in degrees of deleveraging but the graph is quite representative.

In most of the developed economies, bank credit to the private sector decreased significantly after 2008, as shown in Figure 2.15. The total decrease in European banks was close to $6 trillion, which is not a negligible amount. There was a relatively modest increase in US banks but it was too small for the size of the US banking sector. As all of this was happening in the West, a reverse process was taking place in other parts of the world. Led by China, domestic bank credit to the private sector in fast-growing emerging economies expanded considerably from the early 2000s and did not change course after the 2008 crisis.

The increase in China alone was more than twice the decrease in Europe. This has to do with the cuts in direct credit by Western banks to emerging markets and also unique economic and political developments in these countries. In short, the

Figure 2.15: Change in bank credit to private sector (2008–2017)

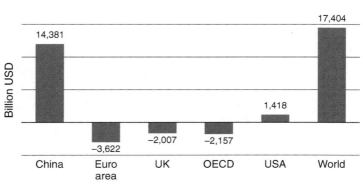

Data sources: World Bank [6] and BIS [1]

effects of new regulations aiming at lower bank leverage seem to have been limited within the European markets and global growth in debt has continued.

Figure 2.16 shows growth in global debt by type and amount. From 2000 to 2008, the annual rate of growth in global debt was 12% while global GDP had grown at about 8%. All types of debt (household, corporate, government and financial) grew at remarkable rates during the period, at the end of which the financial crisis hit, when total debt was $174 trillion. Since then, debt has continued to grow at a slower rate of about 6% – still reaching an all-time record of about $270 trillion – but GDP growth has also slowed down to about 3% per year. This is because most of the developed economies had entered into recession after the crisis.

Figure 2.16: Global debt

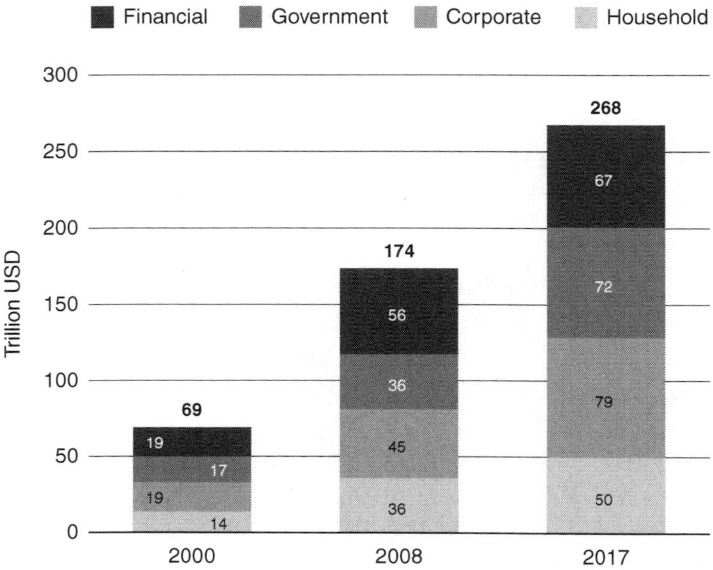

Data sources: World Bank [6], BIS [1] and IMF [2]

From 2008 to 2017, household debt and debts of financial institutions have continued to grow, but this time at relatively lower rates than the pre-crisis rates. Share of household debt in total debt has not changed much. Share of financial debt has declined from 32% to 25% of the total, reflecting the impact of new stricter regulation of bank capital and liquidity. On the other hand, government debt has doubled from $36 to $72 trillion (an increase from 20% to 27% of the total), largely to finance fiscal spending to stimulate economies out of recession and also partly to finance the indirect costs of bailouts of large financial institutions. The more peculiar development is seen in the market for corporate debt. Although bank credit to domestic private sector and foreign corporate borrowers increased by about $17 trillion from 2008 to 2017 (Figure 2.15), total corporate debt worldwide had doubled from $45 to $79 trillion by the end of 2017. The difference is largely due to increasing bond issues by corporations and also partly due to expanding non-bank credit intermediation. In 2017, bond financing made up more than 25% of new corporate debt, which is the highest percentage seen since the early 1990s. A new type of shadow banking is seen in private equity firms, which have increasingly become more like credit suppliers than equity investors. If this trend continues, those firms are better called "private debt" rather than "private equity".

With all the numbers put together, we see a picture of a world economy where debt is growing faster than income, and the gap is widening further. The phrase "this time is different" was often used after the 2008 crisis to point out that it was different from previous crises in history. It may or may not have been true then but, as far as excessive indebtedness is concerned, this time is no different from 2008. Debt is everywhere and on the rise, as before. On the other hand, considering the changing nature of debt markets (partial replacement of bank credit by market-based debt and the rise of new types of shadow banking), this time may also said to be different in critical aspects. Time will tell if this change is for the better or worse but early signs are not very comforting. Shares of low-grade bonds in new bond issues seem to be increasing and several jurisdictions allow certain types of debt to be hidden in the small print of footnotes to financial reports. More on these later.

Another important global development since 2008 has been further concentration of debt in a few countries. Figure 2.17 shows the debt trends in four major economies since the 1970s. As of 2018, the US, China, Japan and the UK constitute more than half of total global debt. It is difficult to predict how long it may last but Japan and the UK seem to have slowed down growth of debt after 2008. More strikingly, the US and China alone make up about 40% of the total and their debt levels are increasing relentlessly. This debt is both domestic debt and also lending to foreign entities. In recent years, China has been pouring credit into African and other countries on the Silk Road. The world now has two competing poles of extreme financial risk and instability. And most issuances of debt are denominated in a single currency, the US dollar, regardless of country of origin. It is complex and confusing, to say the least.

Figure 2.17: Total debt by country

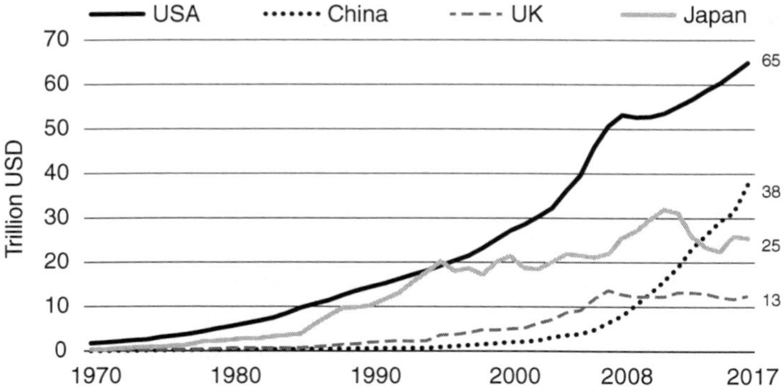

Data sources: World Bank [6], BIS [1] and IMF [2]

Despite all regulatory attempts to control its excess growth, debt continues to grow. This is simply because there is demand for debt. If regulation constrains certain types of debt, market players quickly design new types to replace them. This is a general weakness with our overall approach to regulation, which aims to ascertain that lived problems do not recur. This is usually done merely by regulating institutions and instruments and with no or little consideration of underlying causes of problems. Regulating bank balance sheets alone cannot solve the global problem of too much debt. The story of debt markets after 2008 is a case in point. A functional approach to regulation would be much more effective.

Too little equity

Bonds and equities are the two main sources of market-based capital for corporations. New equity can be raised through an initial public offering (IPO) of shares of private companies to be listed on a stock exchange, or through a secondary public offering (SPO) of newly issued shares of already listed companies. Both are additional new external capital being injected into the company. Corporate bonds can be similarly issued through a public offering, or through direct placement to a small number of investors. Both listed public and unlisted private companies can issue bonds. As a form of debt, bonds represent an alternative to bank credit. Choices between debt and equity determine the "capital structure" of a company.

For more than two decades, corporations have preferred debt financing over equity financing. Figure 2.18 shows the annual amounts raised through bond issues and IPOs/SPOs since the 1990s. The first panel shows total issues by financial institutions and non-financial corporations, the second shows issues by non-financial corporations alone. In both cases, annual amounts raised by bond issues is around four times that by equity issues. The low level of IPO proceeds is particularly striking.

Figure 2.18: New bond and equity issues

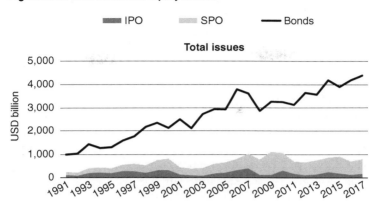

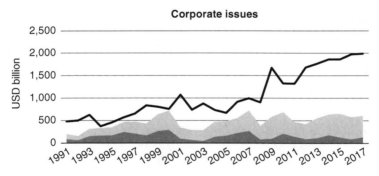

Data source: OECD [3]

Companies do not seem to like going public. Similar patterns are seen in developed and emerging markets alike. There is a global preference for debt.

A more interesting and somewhat alarming trend is dramatic declines in the number of companies listed on public stock exchanges. While everything about finance was growing, the total number of public companies worldwide decreased by about 900 between 1995 and 2017. Figure 2.19 shows the changes in number of listed companies since 2000 in five heavyweight countries of finance. There are significantly fewer listed companies in the US, UK, France and Germany. The most dramatic decline is seen in the US equity markets, where the number declined to 4,336 companies in 2017 from 6,917 companies in 2000 (this number was at its peak of 8,090 in 1996). The US equity market has been the biggest in the world for a century and it has been the textbook from which many other countries learned the business of stock exchanges. Therefore, reasons for this dislike of listing must be seriously studied. Similar falls are seen in Germany, France and the UK.[11]

In contrast to these changes in the West, the number of listed companies has increased remarkably in China and Japan in the East. The number of public companies in China (3,485) is likely to surpass that in the US (4,336 and counting down) in the near future. The Tokyo Stock Exchange now has more listed companies than all of the exchanges in the UK, Germany and France combined. From its past experiences, Japan knows best how sole dependence on debt can be destructive. And, as far as equity markets are concerned, it is as if China's financial sector is living the 1970s and 1980s of the US financial industry.

Figure 2.19: Number of publicly listed companies

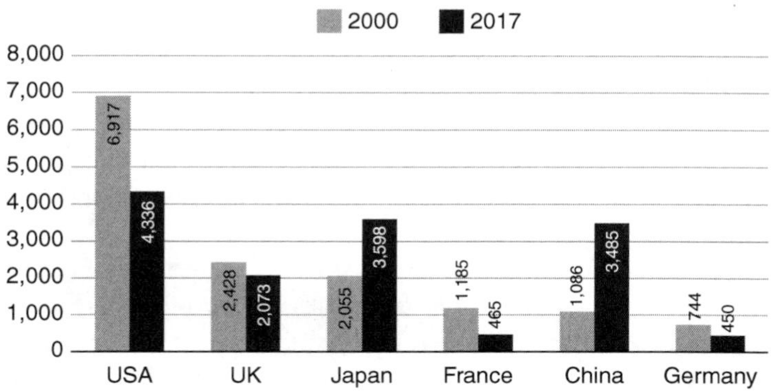

Data source: OECD [3]

There are several reasons for the decline in the number of public companies in Western economies. First of all, companies no longer believe that their companies are fairly valued on stock markets. Factors such as investor short-termism, algorithmic trading technologies and costly regulatory burdens have changed the business models of stock exchanges in ways not welcomed by corporations. As a result, private companies are reluctant to go public, and public corporations may want to delist to go back to being a private company again. In recent years, "going private" is popularly done by companies buying back their own shares of stock in the market, often with borrowed funds. Huge volumes of mergers and acquisitions (M&A) during the past few decades, especially in the US, have also reduced the number of public companies. Merger of two public companies, or acquisition of a public company by another public company, results in one public company at the end of the transaction. As in most share buybacks, M&As are also often financed with debt. Either path to going private means more debt and less equity at the end.

A typical lifecycle of a corporation or a finance version of the American dream begins with a startup financed first by venture capitalists or by family and friends, and then by private equity investors until the company eventually becomes mature enough to go public. However, in recent years, the story has been disrupted by cash-rich mega corporations buying out small young companies before they can live long enough to see the day of a public offering. For example, since 2010, Google is said to have acquired one technology startup per week. There are about five times as many acquisitions as IPOs. For the acquirer, the buyout makes sense if the acquired company contributes added value but it may also turn out to be a waste. In either eventuality, however, potential competitors are captured early. Net socioeconomic welfare impact of this phenomenon of "big fish eating small fish" is not clear but it certainly dries up the entrepreneurial pool feeding the future of equity markets.

Setting all this aside, an immediate reason why firms may prefer debt over equity is that, in most countries, tax codes and securities laws favor debt financing. For corporate income tax purposes, interest payments on debt are treated as a tax-deductible expense but dividend payments on equity are not. For personal income tax purposes, however, both interest income and dividend income are similarly taxed. This asymmetry is effectively an indirect government subsidy for the cost of debt to companies. In OECD countries, the average effective tax rate on equity is 10% higher than that on debt financing. As for securities laws and regulations, in almost all jurisdictions of the world, reporting, disclosure and governance requirements are incomparably more burdensome and costly for equity issuers than for bond issuers. Publicly listed companies are overtasked and overcharged.

Debt financing is easy but equity financing is hard. It is not natural but we have made it so. Can all of the above facts justify or rationalize the excessive growth of global debt and retreat of equity in developed economies? They certainly cannot. Historically, excessive debt has always ended in insolvency because it comes with a unique financial risk that cannot be controlled or hedged away by the borrower.

For the period after 2000, Figure 2.20 shows graphs of some simple measures of financial risk implied by global debt. The numbers are the same as before: GDP is total global GDP and equity is the total market value of listed companies. Going from the "more normal" to "less normal", global equity and GDP move in a parallel fashion and the ratio of equity to GDP has generally fluctuated in a narrow range between 0.7 and 1.0. This is except for sudden temporary market crashes as in 2008, when the ratio hit an all-time low of 0.47. Without any implication about the absolute level of equity values, the parallel between company values and GDP is "normal" because we would still like to believe that market valuations reflect economic activity, at least to some extent most of the time.

Figure 2.20: Debt versus equity

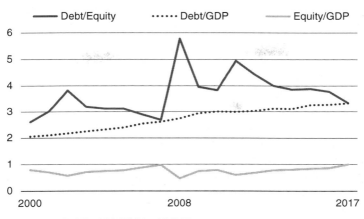

Data sources: World Bank [6], BIS [1] and IMF [2]

The real question is then about the boom-and-bust periods in stock market prices, which cannot be explained by changes in real economic activity. Disconnect between income and stock prices is only possible when there is financial euphoria supported by debt. The joy of rising stock prices triggers more investment in stocks and that requires more borrowing collateralized by the new higher stock values, or other valuable property. Everybody knows it is irrational behavior but they do it anyway. The result is seen in the graph of debt/equity ratios in the figure. Arithmetically, this ratio goes down when equity values go up, and vice versa. When it becomes more difficult to service existing debt and new debt sources dry up, fire sales of collateral follow, causing a sudden market crash. This is exactly the pattern of destruction witnessed in 2008. Equity values came down by more than 30% globally and people lost their homes and pensions. After the crash, debt became available again and markets recovered but it was no relief for people who had lost their wealth just a year before. It is tragicomic that the pre-2008 pattern is being repeated after only a few years.

From 1980 to 2018, the real rate of growth in global GDP was around 3.5% per year. In other words, a GDP of $81 trillion (the level in 2017) can generate a historical-average real value-added ("net profit") of about $3 trillion. During the same period, the real rate of interest has been 2.5% in the US, which is probably lower than in most other countries. This means an annual real interest payment of at least $7 trillion on a principal of $270 trillion globally. The world does not have the financial capacity to service its debt and, to make the problem worse, the ratio of debt to GDP keeps increasing. As Figure 2.20 shows, it has increased from 200% in 2000 to more than 300% of global GDP in 2017. Existing debt cannot be serviced without "producing" more new debt.

Data since 2008 shows that all regulatory and policy attempts at deleveraging did not work. While it is true that balance sheets of bigger banks (those that can cause systemic risks) were made somewhat safer, there were also two unintended consequences. The first was increased non-bank domestic credit by smaller and less regulated institutions in the advanced economies, replacing reduced bank credit. The second was channeling credit through "related parties" located in "financial centers" to bypass stricter regulation of foreign credit. In the East, China's debt, for example, more than quadrupled after 2007, not only as ordinary bank credit but also more via unregulated shadow banking and off-balance-sheet borrowing by local governments. The global approach to debt turned out to be only a game of "name changing", with no change in reality. An equity-to-debt ratio of three, as shown in Figure 2.20, means that 75% of public companies' assets are effectively owned by lenders and creditors. High leverage can probably be seen in private companies as well.

The world economy is based on too much debt and too little equity, for reasons discussed above. Moral, legal and social aspects of debt and credit, and how excessive indebtedness damages responsible behavior and corporate governance in companies will be discussed later in the book. In principle, debt is not a bad thing because it is a way for the "haves" to increase the purchasing power of the "have nots". Debt turns bad when it becomes "excessive", as is the case in the world today. As a rule of thumb, debt is excessive when there is an inability to pay it back, which is often when there is regulatory inability to follow and understand the events in financial markets. Then it causes economic and social damage. Only economic damage is measurable.

Given global consensus on the nature of the problem, the excessive debt issue naturally triggered several studies since the 2008 crisis, by international organizations and academics. The purpose is to find out about the relation between debt levels and financial meltdowns, and also to estimate the relation between debt and economic welfare. Findings from different samples of countries and time spans are largely similar, and there are no surprises:

- Composition and types of finance matter. More debt financing slows down economic growth and more equity financing boosts economic growth. There may be some small country-specific variations around this average finding. For example, in some countries with poor governance backgrounds, too much equity financing may also reduce growth in the long run. But it is a generally valid conclusion for all times studied.
- Reasonable levels of debt can boost growth in the short run but more debt as a percentage of income becomes a drag on growth after a certain threshold in the long run. It must be noted that the short run ends before the debt matures and the long run starts before the debt is fully paid back.
- The threshold after which more debt slows down growth seems to be 90% for public debt, 90% for corporate debt and 85% for household debt. The precision and future validity of the estimated numbers aside, all studies illustrate the existence of some level beyond which debt becomes dangerous.

- As far as its negative impact on economic growth is concerned, the type of debt also matters. Bank credit is worse than market-based financing such as bonds. Bank credit to households is worse than bank credit to corporations. Excessive bank credit to households seems to be the most destructive, as was the case with home mortgage credits before 2008.
- For advanced and emerging economies alike, the average growth rate of GDP in countries with public debt exceeding 90% of GDP is several percentage points lower than that in other countries with lower debt ratios. This finding is for domestic public debt denominated in local currency. When public debt is external in a foreign currency (as is the case in some emerging markets), GDP growth rate is almost cut in half. This explains the long recession in many countries after the 2008 crisis, when debt migrated from the private sector to the public sector.

The studies are all clear and full of lessons to learn. But there is also a hidden side of excessive debt, which is noticed only after a recession starts, collateral values drop, credit markets become tighter and defaults start. Recessions and default events in many countries after 2008 could have been much milder if the supply of debt had not been suddenly disrupted. Lack of prudence and learned experience hides this dark side of debt. People play "blind and deaf" in good times when money is abundant. But prudent behavior should stop the growth of debt before it is too late. Academic debate about the choice between debt and equity has to continue with proper consideration of today's new facts.

Bad derivatives

Derivatives are not new instruments and various kinds have existed in various markets of the world for at least two centuries. For most of the 19th and 20th centuries, their trading was largely limited with exchange-traded futures contracts on agricultural commodities and a few metals. They were used basically for insurance against undesired price movements in underlying commodities. For instance, a wheat farmer, who does not want a low price for his wheat at harvest time, sells a futures contract now to ensure a good delivery price then. The buying counterparty is often a user of wheat (say, a bakery), who does not want high prices in future purchases of wheat. It is a perfect match of opposite risk exposures and trading parties either already own or will own the underlying commodity. Organized exchanges had rules to prevent speculation by parties who had no links to the underlying assets and also had limits on order sizes to prevent manipulative trades. It was small, simple and safe.

Complex derivative contracts such as options and swaps had limited existence in markets because nobody really knew how to price them properly. This was only until 1973 when two professors, Fischer Black and Myron Scholes, published a seminal paper, in which they developed a rational mathematical model of option pricing. The same year, Robert Merton refined the math behind the model. All three academicians would later receive Nobel prizes in economics. Ever since, the model has been celebrated as the Black–Scholes (or sometimes as the Black–Scholes–Merton) model of option pricing and became the building block of all books and computer software on derivatives pricing. A year later, convinced that options are rationally "pricable" instruments, US law makers opened the door for options trading on the Chicago exchanges and elsewhere. Later, in 1981, the currency swap between IBM and the World Bank is often cited as the start of the over-the-counter swap market. Modern derivatives markets kicked off.

Until the early 1990s, the notional value of derivatives had stayed under $50 trillion, with trade volumes dominated by merchants with direct interest in values of underlying assets, portfolio managers, specialized dealers and necessarily by speculators. The Bank for International Settlements, under its current mandate, was not around yet and the Glass–Steagall Act of 1933 in the US was still in effect. Glass–Steagall was a response to the financial crash of 1929–1930 and prohibited commercial banks offering investment banking services such as insurance, derivatives trading and asset management. During the period when it was effective, the US markets enjoyed stable and productive progress. Then came a strong deregulation wave under Ronald Reagan in the US and Margaret Thatcher in the UK in the 1980s. Policies of deregulation spanned many industries but finance was to change the most. The First Basel Accord was signed in 1988 and became immediately effective in most European jurisdictions. The accord enabled easier cross-border banking and partially rendered possible derivatives trading by banks. However, with Glass–Steagall still in effect in the US, the impact of the Basel accord on global markets was limited. Finally, the Gramm–Leach–Bliley Act in 1999 completely repealed Glass–Steagall. The new law, also known as the Financial Modernization Act, triggered many disruptive changes in finance but two were fundamental. First, separation between commercial and investment banking was removed. Among many other risky ventures now made possible, banks could freely trade derivatives using deposits. Second, although it was also possible since the early 1990s, the new law now made it easier for financial institutions to convert from "ordinary partnerships" to "limited liability corporations". As a result of these changes, banks could make riskier investments and trade riskier products under the stronger legal protection of limited liability. Using the French term, a period of complete "laissez faire, laissez passer" began for banks.

In December 2000, the Commodity Futures Modernization Act (CFMA) was passed in the US. It put a final topping on the cake of the Gramm–Leach–Bliley Act. Not only was free trading of derivatives by banks now possible but also trading of derivatives written on any type of asset imaginable. And this could be done under minimal supervision. The immediate result was an explosion in derivatives markets, shown before in Figure 2.9. As there was no requirement to report OTC trading data to a central data warehouse (or a similar setup), neither financial authorities nor most other people could watch and know what was going on in the markets. Trading opacity continued into the 2008 crash and a few more years thereafter.

In retrospect, we now understand what Warren Buffett meant when he said, in his 2002 letter to shareholders, "derivatives are financial weapons of mass destruction, carrying dangers that, while now latent, are potentially lethal" (2002, 15). Derivatives business since 1990s has been a prime case of bad finance. Two cases will suffice to prove this. For the first case, Figure 2.21 shows spot prices of four major commodities (wheat, oil, gold, copper) before and after December 2000, the birth date of the CFMA. Varying but similar patterns can be observed in all commodities on which derivatives are traded.

For clarity, all prices are standardized at 100 in 1988. Two observations from the figure are immediately striking. First, average levels of all commodity prices have increased after 2000. It may be claimed that part of these increases were related to physical demand and supply but a comparison of levels before and after the CFMA in 2000 would call for a much better explanation than such a simple claim. It is too coincidental to be true. Average price has increased by about 2.5 times since 2000. Secondly and most importantly, volatilities of spot prices have increased markedly more than sixfold since 2000. There cannot be any economic explanation for this phenomenon. It is obvious that increased trading of commodity derivatives has increased the volatility of spot prices. In theory, derivatives are to be used mostly for insurance and hedging purposes and this is supposed to decrease price volatility. But the reality has been just the opposite. There has been too much unnecessary trading of derivatives and this can only be between parties that have nothing to do with the underlying commodities. For example, more than 10–15 times the amount of oil that actually exists is

Figure 2.21: Commodity prices

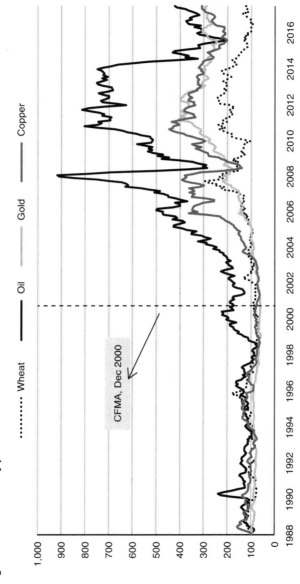

Price = 100 in 1988

Data source: IMF [2]

traded with oil derivatives every year! It has been a costly game between speculative derivatives traders, who would not know or care about any differences between crude oil and orange juice. They are just prices and money can be made on price movements, either up or down! A type of bad financialization.

At a given point in time, the futures price of an asset must be equal to its spot price plus carrying costs to expiry. This is a static view and any deviation from this equilibrium condition triggers correction in either spot price or futures price or both. If futures contracts are on a notional value 10 times bigger than spot availability, it is obvious that the futures price will lead and the spot price will follow (at least, to a large extent). When there is too much derivatives trading, contractual prices on derivatives will inevitably affect spot prices. The problem is that what is "just a price" to a derivatives trader is purchasing power for people. "Financialized" prices of agricultural commodities distorts global income distribution because poorer households and countries spend a bigger percentage of their income on food than richer ones. Such lack of affordability of food translates into a human problem, this time caused not by economic market forces but by financialization. For poorer countries, commodity price fluctuations also cause financial instability and this often results in banking problems. In this game, there is textbook-style "price discovery" but purchasing power is hurt and "value discovery" is forgotten.

The second case, showing how derivatives can be destructive not only for traders but also for the whole economy, concerns credit default swaps and similar instruments. Credit default swaps are particularly interesting to study. A CDS is similar to an insurance contract, providing the insurance buyer protection against specific credit events such as bankruptcy or default. There are many types of CDSs: basic vanilla types, digital CDSs, basket CDSs and portfolio/index CDSs. It is called a credit default "swap" because, as in any swap, there is an exchange of payments between two parties: one party pays a fee ("buys a CDS") and the other party ("selling a CDS") makes a payment contingent on a credit event happening. They are often categorized under the general class of credit derivatives.

There were earlier trades of similar credit derivatives by Bankers Trust but the birth of moderns CDSs is often credited to the JPMorgan bank in 1994. Then, JPMorgan had extended a $5 billion credit to ExxonMobil and did not want to carry the credit risk potentially stemming from Exxon facing punitive damages for its oil tanker's disastrous spill of crude oil near Alaska back in 1989.[12] A team of JPMorgan quantitative analysts engineered a CDS contract to transfer the Exxon credit risk to a party that would be willing to carry it. The European Bank of Reconstruction and Development (EBRD) turned out to be the willing party to sell Exxon CDSs to JPMorgan. In other words, EBRD was the insurer and the bank was the insurance buyer. As a result, JPMorgan could effectively cut the reserves that banking regulations required it to hold against Exxon's default, and its balance sheet was thus improved. On the other hand, EBRD was not subject to any reserve requirements and thus could carry an "Exxon risk" on its balance sheet at a lower cost than JPMorgan. This was a case of pure regulatory arbitrage and both parties won. The bank was freed of credit risk (presuming EBRD would be able to pay in case of Exxon's default) and the cost of high reserves, and EBRD received CDS payments from the bank.

The pros and cons of the Exxon deal may be up for discussion but it could not be a cause of much additional systemic risk for the economy. Total credit risk remained the same, only carriers of risk were switched. As such, it was acceptable. But the CDS story did not stop there. The Commodity Futures Modernization Act of 2000 in the US specifically declared that CDSs are neither futures contracts nor securities. Hence, neither the CFTC nor the SEC had any authority to regulate them. Thereafter, derivatives business transformed into a high-speed avalanche.

It may have been sensible for JPMorgan to seek insurance protection on its credit exposure to Exxon. But how about a totally unrelated party, who has no credit exposure to Exxon, buying insurance against Exxon's default? How about people who have no mortgage debt buying CDSs on mortgage-backed securities? This is, more or less, exactly what AIG (American Insurance Group) did by selling half a trillion dollars-worth of CDSs on not only mortgage products but also on several other assets to people who had no direct economic interest in the underlying value. As a result, the notional value of CDSs globally grew from less than half a trillion dollars before 2000 to more than $60 trillion in 2008.

Notional values of credit default swaps and commodity futures since 2000 are shown in Figure 2.22. For these derivatives, the concept of notional value is specifically important. Unlike other derivatives, notional value is often equal to potential credit exposure in CDS positions. For commodity derivatives, how excessive derivative positions in commodities could distort spot

Figure 2.22: Notional values of CDSs and commodity derivatives

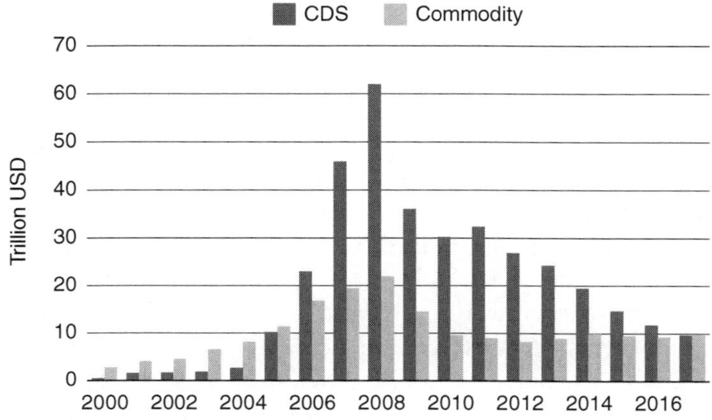

Data sources: BIS [1] and WFE [7]

prices was explained before. Both series peak around the global financial crisis in 2008.

A person can reasonably buy fire insurance on their own house. If a fire burns down the house, then the insurance company indemnifies. Now imagine dozens of unrelated people, people who do not even know where the house is, buying fire insurance on this one house and the house being destroyed by a fire. Further imagine thousands of people buying insurance not only on their own homes but also on each and every other house in an economy. There will be a huge collective interest in a big fire destroying all of the insured houses! But there is a small catch to this scenario in that no insurance company can withstand such an event. The inevitable end is a financial crash. Obviously, this scenario is only imaginary insofar as home insurance is concerned, but CDS trading on mortgage credits and CDOs before the 2008 crash was not really much different. Bet on a chain of bets and speculation on a chain of speculations. We all lived the final scene of the movie.

Overgrowth of derivatives is about how well-educated and smart people can be very stupid when greed is fed into herd psychology. History is rich in such cases. After all his life savings were wiped out in the famous South Sea Bubble scandal in early 1700s, Isaac Newton, who was not only one of the most brilliant scientists ever but also the manager of the Royal Mint at the time, bewailed that he "could calculate the motions of the heavenly bodies but not the madness of people" (Francis, 1850). By today's standards, Newton was a victim of a very simple scam and was naively "phished" by the behavior of other smart people around him. If he had lived today, he probably would not have been pulled into buying shares of South Sea lookalikes but he would certainly have been enchanted by the mathematics of derivatives and complex trading algorithms. Today, in the financial industry, there may be few people close to Newton's brilliance as a scientist but certainly there are many stunt actors playing Newton. If he could not calculate the madness of "uneducated and naive people" of his century, he certainly could not calculate the madness of "educated and smart people" of our century. Today, Isaac Newton would again retire as a poor person.

Complexity of the system

From one perspective, the financial landscape today is one of ever-increasing debt, a declining role of equity markets, and big derivatives business. From another perspective, it is one of a very complex ecosystem. Markets, institutions, instruments, models and interconnections within the system have all become too complex to describe with any level of adequacy. Size and complexity together constitute a vicious cycle in that complexity enables uncontrolled growth and uncontrolled growth feeds in more complexity. Unless the basic building blocks are properly reconsidered, it is almost impossible to tame finance.

For clarity of terminology, complexity exists when the process of intermediation – the basic function of finance – becomes opaque and difficult to trace. Activities which have nothing or little to do with financial intermediation are more easily disguised in more complex setups. Complexity makes it more difficult to foresee the consequences of decisions and hence increases the probability of bad financial decisions. It becomes hard to distinguish bad from good, and dangers become visible only when it is too late. On the other hand, it is sometimes argued that, in some ways, complexity may be good because it fosters innovation. Innovation is valuable when it simplifies life or when it produces new opportunities for happiness. During the last few decades, few innovations in finance have served either of these purposes and, to the contrary, most have only made finance more complex. So the argument may be more valid beyond finance.

Financial instruments have become increasingly more complicated since 1990s. Credit derivatives and other exotic products are complicated products for the average person. But financial professionals with appropriate expertise can have a clear knowledge of how they are structured and how they work. As such, a complicated product is not a cause of system complexity as long as experts are trading them. Complexity starts when ordinary people start trading complicated products, the consequences of which they have no clue about. If the seller is an expert and the buyer is a novice, there is a problem. If both sides are novices, there is a bigger problem. If a small number of experts and a large number of novices are interconnected on a global financial and trade network, there is a global problem. In the worst scenario, when most of the experts are falsely thought to be experts, then we have a problem of complexity leading to the probability of a financial disaster.

An illustrative case of complexity is presented by Célérier and Vallée (2014), who identified more than 55,000 structured financial products sold to retail customers in 16 European countries between 2002 and 2010. They use three joint measures of product complexity: the number of words in the product description, number of features in the payoff formula and number of possible payoffs. An example in the paper is a product called Vivango sold to retail customers (mostly households) by the French Post Office Bank in 2010:

Vivango is a 6-year maturity product whose final payoff is linked to a basket of 18 shares (largest companies by market capitalization within the Eurostoxx 50). Every year, the average performance of the three best-performing shares in the basket, compared to their initial levels is recorded. These three shares are then removed from the basket for subsequent calculations. At maturity, the product offers guaranteed capital of 100%, plus 70% of the average of these performances recorded annually throughout the investment period. (2010, 7)

Vivango would probably have a rating of low complexity. Even then, what can the customers of "La Banque Postale" make of a bond product with an uncertain contingent return? Why is the bank offering such a complicated product to households?[13] Neither the sellers nor the buyers seem to have wondered why. On the contrary, both number and complexity of retail structured products have consistently increased since the 1990s. Banks have offered more of such products in periods of low interest rates and when there is more intense competition in the sector. Most importantly, the more complex the product is, the higher is the profit to the bank and also the lower the return to the investor. Clearly, investors would not have bought these products if they had understood them. This is a typical case of a zero-sum financial game with a positive sum for the industry and a commensurate negative sum for the investors. It is a case of regulatory inability to protect investors from "misinformation" hidden under complexity. The result is continual growth in complexity, and risks piling up.

Most people consider collateralized debt obligation (CDO), and all its versions, as complex because they have complicated structures. A CDO is designed by bundling a group of loans (mortgage, car, student and project finance loans, corporate bonds, credit card receivables and the like) in order to issue a new security called a "CDO note". The note is broken into tranches by seniority and with varying coupons. Investors can buy any tranche. The lowest rated junior tranche receives the highest coupon but, in case of default in the original loans, gets wiped out first. The highest rated senior tranche receives the lowest coupon but gets wiped out only after all of the subordinate tranches are depleted. In the middle is the mezzanine tranche. The emerging structure is such that holders of CDO notes have a claim on the issuer of the note, who in turn has a claim on the initial group of loans. It is a claim on a claim. It gets more intriguing when a group of CDOs (instead of loans) are resecuritized into yet another CDO, this time called "CDO squared", which now implies a chain of three sequential claims on the same cash flows. Indeed, CDOs have complicated cash flow structures.

The payoff to CDO investors naturally depends on the joint performance of all the original loans, which depends largely on the correlations of defaults among these loans and maybe slightly on probabilities of individual defaults. This is where an unexpected consequence of complexity pops up. In normal times, as during the four decades after the Second World War, correlations of defaults among different loans of all types were quite low. These are calculated with complicated mathematical methods (such as copula models) and historically correlations do not seem to change much, yielding reliable estimates. This evidence was hence a reason for comfort of CDO quantitative analysts and issuers. Until the 1990s, looking at historical data, nobody could imagine a nationwide wave of defaults on mortgage loans in the US. But it happened during the 2007–2008 crash. And when it happened, all of those previously low correlations of defaults increased fast, to much higher degrees. The models could not predict the crash because they were based on assumptions of constant correlations. Defaults spread and CDOs (and, indeed, all financial products blindly based on historical correlations) turned into junk.

This was a case of complicated mathematical models enabling issuance of complicated financial products, consequences of which are not fully understood by either the sellers or the buyers. In an article published by *Evening Standard*, Michael Lewis (2008) correctly pointed out that

> [CEO of Bear Stearns] plays bridge and [CEO of Merrill Lynch] golfs while their firms collapse, not because they don't care that their firms are collapsing, but because they don't know their firms are collapsing. Across Wall Street, CEOs have made this little leap of faith about the manner

in which their traders are making money, because they don't fully understand what their traders are doing.

This is one of many ways in which complexity in finance breeds potential hazards.

Complexity of financial products and their background mathematical models is only a small part of the problem. In the bigger picture, the whole intermediation process itself has evolved into a complex network of trade transactions and information flows, which are almost impossible to trace and oversee. Figure 2.23 gives an oversimplified diagrammatic summary of the part of financial intermediation often referred to as asset management. It excludes basic commercial banking (business of deposit collection and credit extension), regulatory processes, international flows and many finer details of asset management itself. Including all in one chart would be very difficult to draw and require a very big sheet of paper. A simple chart is enough to make the point (Figure 2.23).

The fundamental function of financial intermediation is to channel household savings into productive uses in the real economy. It is about optimal transformation of savings into real investments in order to increase economic welfare for all. Financial regulations and rules of corporate governance are all designed to have an intermediation process conducive to both the formation of capital at the household level and also its optimal allocation at the corporate investment level. Users of capital are responsible for making good investments and owners of capital should be able and willing to see how their savings are being used. That is why public securities markets exist and why corporate governance is the essence of good public policy and regulation in finance. The model of free markets becomes problematic when owners of capital and its users cannot "communicate" over a proper intermediation platform.

As seen in Figure 2.23, there are at least three layers of intermediaries even in a simple, straightforward transaction of

Figure 2.23: Process of financial intermediation

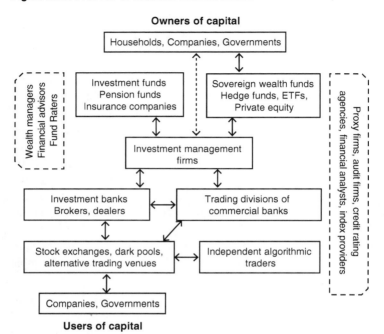

a person choosing a pension fund and the fund working with an investment bank to access the stock market. Pension fund, investment bank and the stock exchange are between the owner and user of capital. Depending on the range of services offered by the intermediaries, the number of firms involved in the process may increase to four, five and even six. And this does not include the "auxiliary" services provided by audit firms, advisors, credit rating agencies and others written in the dotted boxes in Figure 2.23. It also does not include "intruders" such as proxy firms, index providers and algorithmic robo-traders. Arrows designate flows of money. As in a Turkish saying, "everybody has a hand in everybody's pockets".

Figure 2.23 clearly shows that the process of securities intermediation has become very complex with multiple layers of interconnected intermediaries engaged in activities that often do not have much to do with intermediation. Complexity has further intensified over time. In the final analysis, however, much of such trading activity must build on households' savings – on other people's money. Intermediary firms have their own business models and naturally they all aim at maximizing their own profits. When the balance sheets of the trade-level intermediaries (investment banks, commercial banks, stock exchanges) in the chart are read, it will be seen that most of their financial assets are the financial liabilities of other intermediaries, and vice versa. What do these huge volumes of trading between intermediaries have to do with the real owners and ultimate users of capital? No wonder finance has grown so much and turned into a complex web of business models and objectives. No wonder economies of scale have never been achieved in financial intermediation.

There are many industry-specific factors behind the increase in size and complexity of intermediation but, in search of a solution to problems of finance, it is useful to look back at some transformational trends and changes in the real corporate world and in public markets over the last 40 years. Before 1980s, more than 80% of publicly traded shares of corporate equity in the US were held by households. In other words, the majority of shareholders were individuals. If a person did not like the performance of a company, they could sell their shares on the stock exchange and buy shares of other companies they like better. Apparently, such "exits" were not frequent as the average holding period of stocks in the US exchanges was around 5–6 years from the 1950s to the 1980s. Shareholders were "loyal" partners. This may be a good thing, or a bad thing, depending on how engaged these long-term shareholders were in monitoring corporate management. In any case, owners of capital had a one-step path to users of capital.

Since the 1980s, in the US and most advanced economies, ownership structures of public companies have changed significantly into a more concentrated structure. By the 1990s, institutional investors had already replaced individual investors and became the major shareholders of public corporations. Institutional investor holdings of US exchange-traded equities, as a proportion of the total, increased from 30% in 1985 to more than 85% in 2017. Households are now "indirect" investors in equities through mutual funds, pension funds and other intermediaries. The rise of institutional investors has transformed old structures of corporate control and killed the textbook concept of "shareholder value". These changes have probably been the most foundational changes in free-market capitalism from the Second World War into the current century. They have also been background enablers of the enormous growth of size and complexity in finance.

Figure 2.24 shows the growth of assets under management by major institutional investors between 2000 and 2017. They include insurance companies, pension funds and mutual funds (also known as unit trusts, or investment funds). As of mid-2017, total assets reached about $88 trillion globally, up from $25 trillion in 2000. On top of this, when sovereign wealth funds with $12 trillion, hedge funds with $3.5 trillion, ETFs ("exchange-traded funds") with about $4.5 trillion and private equity funds with $4 trillion are added, total assets under management reach about $110 trillion in 2017.[14] Except for relatively minor shares of private wealth management and direct investment in real estate, most of household savings are managed by institutional funds today. This is a market structure with critical fundamental implications.

Dominance of institutional investors in corporate equity has inevitably separated asset ownership from corporate management. The textbook description of the agency–principal problem has changed into an agency–agency–principal problem, or maybe into a non-problem. Since households are no longer

Figure 2.24: Financial assets managed by institutional investors

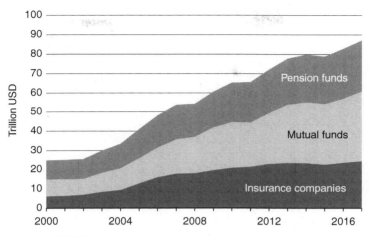

Data source: OECD [3]

direct shareholders, they cannot act on their own interest to monitor corporate performance. The ownership function is now exercised by institutional investors, or by the other intermediaries in the system. The problem is that, since these intermediaries have their own profit-maximizing business models and trading strategies, the way they exercise the ownership function can often be different from how households would engage on their own. For instance, if corporate performance is not satisfactory, households can sell their shares and walk away. Funds cannot behave so freely because their sales would be in large volumes and this would depress prices, resulting in further losses. Instead, institutional investors use their ownership power to force corporations to deliver good performance, and good performance usually means higher stock prices as soon as possible. This is a push for short-termism. Also expressed as "earnings management" or "managerial myopia", short-termism is excessive focus by corporate managers, fund managers and analysts on short-term results and sacrifice of long-term firm value – forget the future and get good results this quarter. This is possible only with more borrowing to "cash up" current earnings, or using all of the suitable small-print footnotes of financial reporting rules to report higher profit numbers now (and consequently much lower numbers in the future). In the meantime, higher stock prices mean higher bonuses for corporate managers and for fund managers. The ultimate result is destruction of the long-term wealth of actual owners of capital, the households.[15] Households did not save and entrust the financial industry with their money for this.

This behavior is more often seen in actively managed mutual funds, and hedge funds in particular. Aggressive ownership engagement is a core part of the business models of these funds. On the other hand, there are also passive funds, or "index funds", which do nothing but build portfolios mimicking a published market index. Trillions of dollars have flowed from active funds to passive funds since 2008, and these funds are increasingly in the form of ETFs, or some variant of ETFs. They can be grounded on broad-based market indexes such as the S&P 500 and the MSCI indexes, or combinations of sectoral indexes such as technology and banking indexes. In the business models of passive funds, ownership engagement has no role; it is just an unnecessary cost item. There is no relevance of individual company valuations and no trace of corporate governance in their trading strategies. They just follow an index.

Another problem is the fact that sectoral classification of corporations may be an important factor in valuations by financial analysts. Regardless of fundamental value drivers, some sectors may be valued more favorably than others. Some years ago, the analyst community was trying to figure out whether Amazon was a bookseller or an internet platform. It took Apple years to convince financial analysts that it was more than a mere hardware vendor. How can a given company's value change with a reclassification in a different sector? It seems arbitrary.

Last but not least is the bigger issue of index inclusion. Some companies (and some countries) are included in market indexes and some are not. This is decided by index providers. The problem is that if a company is not included in an index it cannot be a part of investment by passive indexed funds, and it will probably be outside of the sphere of interest of actively managed funds as well. This is simply because the company is not perceived as being important enough to be included in an index. Unfortunately, most small young companies fall in this category and hence institutional investors do not have much interest in small companies. As a result, smaller companies are not easily able to access capital markets. Regulatory hurdles for small companies come on top of this market fact. Winding the clock back, yesterday's dwarfs but today's giants like Microsoft and Apple would probably have a hard time finding financing had they started up today.[16]

In parallel to changing business models and increasing complexity of investment management, we have also witnessed profound changes in market infrastructures over the last two decades. There have been several mergers and acquisitions among stock exchanges, both vertical and horizontal. Today, there are many cases of a holding company owning several exchanges and its own shares being listed in one or more of those exchanges. Furthermore, revenue sources of stock exchanges have shifted away from IPO/SPO services and more towards trading services for derivatives and any other "profitably tradable" product. Share of IPO/SPO service revenues in total earnings of stock exchanges has steadily declined since the turn of the century. Under their new business models, stock exchanges do not seem to like stocks anymore! Who cares about IPOs?

The last two decades have also seen extensive market fragmentation. Investment banks have largely retreated from exchanges and now prefer trading on alternative off-exchange platforms. Today, about half of all trading of exchange-listed stocks in the US and Europe takes place on platforms outside of exchanges. And more than 40% of all stock trading flows through "dark pools" where, unlike exchanges, pre-trade data about buy and sell positions is not available to the public. The street jargon is "dark trading" versus "lit trading". Inner transaction details of dark trading are not available to market supervisors in real time and this is in sharp contrast to lit trading in exchanges.

Another disruptive trend in stock markets has been the rise of algorithmic and high-frequency trading (HFT) and recently it is also spreading into the bond markets. HFT is basically an intra-day trading strategy commanded by a computer algorithm, which produces buy/sell orders at very high speeds (fractions of a second) to capture a very small profit on every trade. The strategy is based on detecting what other traders are doing (or trying to do) and then moving in faster. It is a computer tool to make money on trade flows only and economic values of traded assets have no relevance whatsoever. Even the names of securities being traded are irrelevant. Without any relation to the quality of assets, HFT-type trading can cause massive movements in asset prices simply as a result of liquidity. Numbers called "price" and "quantity" are all that matter. Not much knowledge of finance and economics is needed. Today, HFT trading has taken hold and makes up more than 75% of all equity trading volume in the US markets. It is fair to say that "price discovery" in the short run is largely done by computers. But then do those prices fairly and truly represent the values of assets and companies?

It is estimated that HFT, passive ETFs and equity-linked options make up more than 90% of all equity trading volume in the US and more than 70% in European markets. In the rest of the world, these proportions are much smaller at around 10–20% but are increasing fast. And, as mentioned above, about half of this volume is in the form of off-exchange dark trading. Wolfe (1930, 11) was correct when he said: "they sell and buy. And nobody ever asks them why". If he lived today, he might have rephrased his words as: "And nobody ever asks them why [and where]". There are too many traders on price but too few investors in value.

The results are not nice. The average stock holding period in the US has notably declined from an average of 5-6 years until the 1980s down to less than three months in 2015. As more trading means more revenue for exchanges, share turnover ratios (ratio of value of shares traded to market cap) have increased from less than 20% before the 1990s to more than 120% in 2017. More trading is not a bad thing because it provides liquidity. At the same time, however, the ratio of shares traded to amount of new equity raised (via IPOs and SPOs) has increased from less than 20 times before early 1990s to about 100 times today. For example, in 2017, the total volume of equity trading globally was about $82 trillion and total new funds raised by corporations was only $800 billion. Trading is fine but then what are stock markets for in the first place? If companies cannot raise enough equity capital through markets, then stock exchanges are not doing a good job. Excessive trading is also evident in the markets of China and Japan, despite growing numbers of IPOs at the same time.

All of the above is really no more than a summary description of how complex the process of intermediation between households (owners of capital) and corporations (users of capital) – only one segment of the overall financial industry – has become. But it still shows that the distance between households and corporations – which is ideally supposed to be transparent and "manageable" – has increased over an almost untraceable complex path. This has and can lead to many unintended consequences. For example, the pension money of an average family in any country may eventually end up financing an undesirable investment in any other part of the world. Alternatively, it may also end up being used as margin for derivatives trading or as collateral in securitizations by intermediaries. Furthermore, this may be the case despite a process of perfect regulatory compliance and a clear purpose to the contrary.

Complex systems change much faster than regulations and institutions can adapt. In our case, unleashed financial technology can engineer and market almost any risk-return package under a very sophisticated title, which regulators and rating agencies often cannot fully comprehend on time. Indeed, innovation of complex financial products may be an unplanned market reaction to regulation. Financial engineers play cat and mouse with regulators. Despite this imbalance between "industry talent" and "regulatory talent", the response of governments has been in the form of increasing the sizes of regulators and of designing similarly complex regulation. A case in point is the length and level of detail of the Dodd-Frank Act in the US in 2010. A new and big "industry of compliance" has emerged as a result. Compliance is costly but compliance to complex regulation is more costly with a side "benefit" of more easily disguising misbehavior under seemingly complete conformity. It should not require much wisdom to predict that regulating complexity with complexity will lead to instability and crises in the long run. Hence, it is no surprise that supervisors, even in the most developed markets of the world, became aware of many types of risk and financial misbehavior only after they led to the crisis of 2008. Murphy's law of "Whatever can go wrong, will go wrong" may be tailored to a financial context as "Whatever can go wrong in finance, will go wrong to a greater extent when complexity is involved".

Resistance to change

A synopsis of the history of economics as a discipline may give a useful perspective of the world of finance today. The birth of classical economics in the West is usually credited first to Adam Smith, author of *The Wealth of Nations* in 1776 and later to David Ricardo (1817), who was inspired by Smith's "invisible hand" governing free markets and added some analytical rigor to the concept. In the classical approach, markets are as good as they are free from government intervention. Throughout the era of industrial revolution in the 19th century, the classical school failed several times and many social/economic crises were seen. However, economists such as John Stuart Mill, author of *Principles of Political Economy* in 1848, and converted economists like William Stanley Jevons (1879), who tried hard to develop a mathematical model linking economic crises to sunspots, insisted and elaborated on Adam Smith's model of free markets, and neoclassical economics was born.[17]

The neoclassical school was the dogma among most economists for more than 150 years and until the Great Depression of 1929. The great economic collapse shattered most people's faith in free markets and a search started for a model of more government and less free markets. On one hand, there were calls for regulation of money and financial markets. Major new regulations in the US were the Glass-Steagal Act in 1933 followed by the Securities Exchange Act in 1934 and the Banking Act in 1935. On the other hand, there was also an intellectual search for an alternative to neoclassical economics and a new school of thought was born with the publication of *The General Theory of Employment, Interest, and Money* by John Maynard Keynes (1936), and its mathematical interpretation by his contemporary John Hicks (1937). In the Keynesian model, financial markets without regulation are no different from casinos,[18] central banks are to be positioned primarily as "suppliers of money" and partly as an element of financial regulation, and the damage of economic slowdowns can only be mitigated by fiscal policies such as government spending. Printing money during slumps is also fine. Keynesian propositions were widely well received and they have influenced the mindsets of even the most rigorous opponents to varying degrees.

However, economists' beliefs do not seem to change easily. This may be due to slow-changing educational contents, or it may be due to a "closed network" of intellectuals under continual peer influence. Maybe continuous repetition of assumptions turns them into perceived realities, which are then hard to challenge. Whatever the real reasons may be, some economists never gave up on their faith in neoclassical economics. In 1934, while in the midst of the Great Depression, economist Joseph Schumpeter claimed that recessions and even depressions are not bad things and indeed they are necessary corrections in the market economy adjusting to changes in business conditions. And government intervention is not needed because it is actually counterproductive. In its purest form, the Keynesian school did not last too long and neoclassical economics was revived as "monetarism" led by Milton Friedman (1969) at the University of Chicago during 1950s. The basic idea was that proper monetary policy (control of money supply through several policy tools by central banks) is all that is needed to ascertain stable growth and prevent depressions. Fiscal policy can affect economic activity in the short run but it can cause structural problems in the long run.

In the 1960s to 1980s, the neoclassical revival went far beyond Friedman's framework. This took place in two different camps: the macroeconomists ("saltwater" economists) in one and the financial economists ("freshwater" economists) in the other. In an attempt to account for economic slowdowns and unemployment, the presence of market imperfections was now recognized. Because of imperfections, shocks to the economy would cause frictions, which slow down the economy and increase unemployment. Expansionary monetary policy would then step in and help a move out of recession. Compared to the earlier neoclassical models of the previous century, this new model contributed further by mathematically modeling the move from equilibrium to disequilibrium and then prescribing a monetary policy action to move to a new general equilibrium. They are often referred to as "dynamic stochastic general equilibrium" models and strangely labeled as "New Keynesian". For the last 40 years, these models have dominated macroeconomic theory and become primary reference models of central banks and treasuries around much of the world.

Independently and somewhat in rivalry, financial economists were developing their own models of financial markets based on a similar assumption of rational behavior by profit-maximizing traders in perfect markets. Further inspired by the doctoral thesis of French mathematician Louis Bachelier (1900) in the early 1900s about the random behavior of stock prices, the 1960s saw Benoit Mandelbrot (1963) introducing statistical martingales into academic finance and Paul Samuelson (1965) of MIT proving mathematically that properly anticipated prices should fluctuate randomly. These laid the analytical foundations of the celebrated efficient markets hypothesis (EMH) by Eugene Fama of Chicago in 1970. Later revised and refined in minor ways by others, EMH claims that security prices in free markets incorporate and immediately reflect all available relevant information. Tomorrow's prices cannot be predicted because, whenever they are, they will be made quickly unpredictable through trading today. Traders who have earlier access to relevant information will naturally have the advantage of higher profits than others and, in free, competitive markets, the marginal revenue from such trading should be equal to the marginal cost of gathering and processing information. For the first time in history, microeconomics' concept of equilibrium could be tested on real data, an abundant resource in finance. More than two centuries after Adam Smith, a chance to "test the invisible hand" was finally here. Using the subway sign as a model: we saw it, we said it and now we only have to sort it.

A landmark in theoretical economics, jointly attributed to Kenneth Arrow (1963) and Gerard Debreu (1959), shows that, if markets are complete[19] and investors are rational, a competitive equilibrium will be efficient. Financial markets are not technically complete because there are transaction costs, taxes, regulatory costs and sometimes barriers to entry. The theory implies that they can be made "more complete" or "less incomplete" with more free trading activity, higher market liquidity, financial innovation and unrestricted capital flows across market segments and geographical borders. For the last four decades, policy makers, regulators and academia have behaved in line with these ideas. Since the inception of the Nobel prize in economics, all of the economists mentioned above were awarded the prize; they built pricing models that assume market efficiency and these have been widely accepted and used in practice.

So, economics has traveled through a full historical cycle of changes since Adam Smith and ended up on the same old paradigm: the optimal model is free markets with a minimum government role. It was like a perfect manifestation of the saying: "the more things change, the most they stay the same". Ideas stayed the same but there were two important differences. The first difference is largely due to many advances in mathematical sciences and computing technologies. What Adam Smith or Keynes could describe in long paragraphs could now be presented in elegant mathematical models. Complex relationships, which those pioneers could not even imagine, can now be modeled, computed in seconds and then presented as a financial product. This was a good thing in principle but with a bad consequence. The most influential group of people in finance, both in academia and in practice, are almost blinded by overreliance on complex models, all of which are based only on a tiny subset of mathematics. Solving a mathematical problem is often perceived as a solution to a financial problem, when in fact it has nothing to with real life. London-based mathematician Paul Wilmott (2010, 246), who trains more financial quantitative traders than anyone else in the sector, has said: "There is too much mathematics in this business. I just want people to stop and think for once", and continued: "There are two types of quants – sensible and stupid. Unfortunately, the stupid – the purist, abstract mathematics-loving quants – are in the majority". The finance profession and education are fully occupied with the question of "how" and almost never consider the more fundamental question of "why".

The second difference between the times of Smith, Keynes (and even Friedman) and our time, is that today's economists with identical foundational models do not form a coherent group of people. In the models of New Keynesian macroeconomists, widely used by central banks and treasuries, there are no financial markets. They are all about monetary and fiscal policies pretending that securities markets do not exist. The economic and political elite in general often underestimate the power of financial technology and engineering. Despite all we have lived through in the first two decades of the century, most still believe that, if needed, financial markets can be controlled via central banking and regulation formatted as lists of rules. They still seem to ignore the fact that financial markets can often mitigate any intended impact of monetary policy and financial regulation, which can also produce unpredictable and unintended consequences as in the case of two decades of "Great Moderation" ending with the 2008 crisis. In the models of financial economists, on the other hand, there is no macroeconomics and there is also very little reference to underlying fundamental values in the real economy. They are all about how financial prices – and only prices – are discovered in free markets.

But then why do we have financial crises with increasing frequency and size? Why cannot (most) economists and governments predict (or at least fear) crises? It seems that the default state of these new models is general equilibrium and they are not designed to incorporate factors causing crises. They are all fundamentally flawed and do not fit into new realities. The basic flaw is the assumption of rational investor behavior and resultant market efficiency. To be fair to the profession, there were economists like Hyman Minsky (doctoral student of Schumpeter) and Robert Shiller of Yale, who had the wisdom to discover these problems. Shiller (2000, 2012) produced ample evidence on irrational behavior and popularized the term "irrational exuberance" and Minsky (1982) had many valid descriptions on investor behavior at and around times of financial crises. On this point, it is also meaningful that the 2017 Nobel prize in economics was given to Richard Thaler, who defends that human beings are not "programmed rational agents" whose behavior can be fully described by pure mathematical models (Thaler 2015). Most recently, Paul Romer, co-winner of the 2018 Nobel Prize in economics, describes the neoclassical models as "post-real" models using "incredible identifying assumptions to reach bewildering conclusions" (2016, 2). It is good to hear wise words from academia and, in fact, similar words from business were expressed years ago by Warren Buffett: "I'd be a bum on the street with a tin cup if the markets were always efficient" (Cunningham 2013, 92). Buffett is not a poor person. However, models of mainstream economists are not much affected. There is a strong resistance to change, or a lack of capability to change.

In her visit to the London School of Economics in 2009, Queen Elizabeth II asked why nobody saw the crisis coming, a question in most people's mind. Robert Lucas' (2009) answer the following day was blunt: "Economics could not give useful service for the 2008 crisis because economic theory has established that it cannot predict such crises." Another renowned economist, Thomas Sargent, supported Lucas by saying that such criticisms "reflect either woeful ignorance or intentional disregard of what modern macroeconomics is about" (Rolnick, 2012). So was the macroeconomists' defense.

When asked about the crisis again, Eugene Fama's attitude and answer in a 2010 interview was not much different: "There was nothing unusual about [the 2008 stock market crash]. That was exactly what you would expect if markets were efficient … There is no empirical evidence to suggest that finance was to blame. Instead, finance was a casualty of the crisis." So was the financial economists' defense.

These answers by three of the most knowledgeable and reputable academicians exemplify the strong resistance to change. It is not much different on the policy front either. In a *Financial Times* article, Alan Greenspan (2011) calls for repeal of the new Dodd-Frank regulation and continues:

> The problem is that regulators, and for that matter everyone else, can never get more than a glimpse at the internal workings of the simplest of modern financial systems. Today's competitive markets, whether we seek to recognize it or not, are driven by an international version of Adam Smith's "invisible hand" that is irredeemably opaque. With notably rare exceptions (2008, for example), the global "invisible hand" has created relatively stable exchange rates, interest rates, prices, and wage rates.

With all due respect to the former chairperson, this is like saying: "With rare exceptions (your kid's head being blown off, for example), Russian roulette is a fun game for families." After all that happened in 2008, these are not words we would expect to hear from famous academicians and policy makers. Inherent conceptual and structural flaws in the financial system should not be overlooked by positioning big crises as once-in-75-years events. Maybe economics in its current limits is no longer up to the task.

Adam Smith's and Keynes' books are likely to be reprinted and to reoccupy the bestselling book lists repeatedly every 50 years, every 20 years, every 10 years and so on.

State of the world today

September 2018 marked the tenth anniversary of the collapse of Lehman Brothers, the calendar date marking the 2008 global financial crisis. For the occasion, several conferences were held and reports were published reflecting on the crisis a decade later. One such event at the Brookings Institute[20] gathered Ben Bernanke (chairman of the Fed), Timothy Geithner and Henry Paulson (both were former Secretaries of the Treasury), the top three US bureaucrats fighting the 2008 crisis, in front of several former and current policy makers, regulators, businesspeople and academics. A few conclusions can be drawn from the conversation with the guests, Q & A chats with the audience and more than a dozen research reports presented at the workshops. All agreed that, with timely decisions and actions, the US authorities were successful in the initial step of putting out a huge fire that could have burned down the whole global financial system. However, there was not much talk of how European governments, albeit slower than their American colleagues, also took proper supporting measures to help fight the crisis. There was no mention whatsoever of how China's huge fiscal spending in 2009 and later probably saved the world from a much deeper recession in the aftermath of the crisis.

The Brookings conference and many others' evaluations of the 2008 crisis and its aftermath seem to show that regulators and policy makers believe they have learned their lessons and now know better what to do when a financial crisis erupts again. This is true but also largely about things to do after a crisis happens, not before. There is very little effort to develop policies to prevent crises. The dominant philosophy is still that there is no need for such preventive policies because market players know best and their interest in surviving is enough to ascertain a safe financial system. Models of "dynamic stochastic general equilibrium" and the "efficient markets hypothesis" seem to be deeply rooted in the minds of many, whether they admit it or not.

More disturbing is the fact that policy makers, regulators and market players have started to forget the 2008 crisis and behave as if it never happened. Only eight years after its enactment, there are already attempts to ease some of the regulations under the Dodd-Frank Act in the US and maybe the current political sentiment will ultimately result in repealing the act altogether. This may again be an example of the memoryless property of economic and financial history, which in turn may be linked to natural human psychology. People tend to forget bad memories more easily than good memories. Economic crises breed political populism and then populism grows on economic euphoria, which is suitably pumped up by lax financial regulation.

History shows us that undesirable events can often teach us more than a thousand words of advice. If it were not for the global crisis, we would not be questioning our established models of economics and finance and searching for better models today. If it were not for financial crises, policy makers and regulators would never feel the need to update their policies and rules. After the 2008 crisis, international policy setters and many national governments enacted new laws and regulations to strengthen the financial system and provide better protection for consumers of financial services. The major new regulations were the Dodd–Frank Act in the US, the Basel III regulations in Europe and, more recently, the 2013 Banking Act in the UK. The common feature is a shift of regulatory focus from "microprudential" supervision of individual institutions to a regime of "macroprudential" supervision to monitor systemic risks in the finance industry. The Dodd–Frank Act is the most comprehensive financial reform act since the Glass–Steagall Act in 1933 after the Great Depression and also among similar reform packages in other countries after 2008. The key features were:

- For big banks and other "systemically important financial institutions" (SIFIs), higher capital and liquidity levels are required in order to better absorb losses from credit events and to meet short-notice cash demands in case of bank runs and liquidity shortages in the markets. As of 2018, there were 30 global SIFIs, assessed as such and published by the Financial Stability Board. National authorities have their own lists of "domestic" SIFIs. The big institutions must also run periodic robust "stress tests" of possible vulnerabilities. They are also required to prepare regular resolution plans ("living wills") for orderly liquidation in case of failure without jeopardizing the rest of the financial system and for assessment by supervisors.

- For derivatives trading, all "standardized" OTC derivatives are required to be cleared through central counterparties (CCP) with multilateral netting of risks. This is to replace the huge volumes of bilateral OTC trading before the crisis, which had caused contagious derivative defaults in the 2008 crisis. These CCPs are also required to maintain "data warehouses" of OTC trading transactions and make it publicly available. Further, in order to eliminate chains of speculation, credit default swaps are now limited to trading only by those parties that have identifiable exposures to the default risk of the underlying asset.
- Rules were introduced to prevent money market mutual funds from providing excessive amounts of short-term wholesale funding to non-bank financial institutions. An example is the complete overhaul of the tri-party repo system in the US. This is to prevent "bank runs" on mutual funds, as was the case when Lehman Brothers became insolvent, and to limit the supply of short-term funds to finance long-term positions of big institutions.

Compared to Europe, most of the new regulations were implemented earlier and more effectively in the US. This was due to not only timely moves by the US government but also lack of full political harmony among European countries. At the time, the European Central Bank was not nearly as powerful in the European Union as the Fed was in the US.

Such were the regulatory responses to the 2008 crisis. They show that the specific problems causing the crisis are well understood by all and the new regulations are mostly appropriate. Big banks in the US and Europe were largely deleveraged as desired and now have stronger equity bases. Money market funds in the US are now smaller and safer. Through central data repositories, authorities have timely access to information on derivatives trading activity in OTC markets, at least information on trading of known standardized derivatives. Exuberant speculative trading of CDSs was largely cut from more than $60 trillion in 2008 to about $10 trillion in 2018. Some of the problems of 2008 appear to have been solved.

But what about the known and as yet unknown problems of today? Can we conclude that regulatory responses and subsequent changes in the financial industry since 2008 have made the world of finance a safer and better place? Unfortunately, the answer is no. As memories fade away with time, it becomes easier for political processes to hinder regulatory updates and even to circumvent existing ones. In the US, much of the follow-up regulation required by the Dodd–Frank Act is still unfinished. Recently, although not yet openly expressed, there also seems to be a political desire to gradually repeal the act. Intentions to deregulate are becoming audible in politics in other parts of the world as well. Regulatory responses have been "backward-looking" and, as they keep looking back and lingering, any chances regulators might have had to be forward-looking will be taken away by political influence. In the meantime, market players will find ways around regulation to engage in profitable and risky trades elsewhere. This is an imminent danger, as it has often been since the 1980s.

The global crisis in 2008 was the worst financial crisis of all time. There have always been flaws in economic policy and financial regulation but it is especially disappointing to observe the same flaws after such a calamity. There are two fundamental problems in regulation. First, despite all the initial enthusiasm after 2008 to cooperate globally, regulation is still fragmented both domestically and internationally. This results in regulatory arbitrage, and domestic politics resisting international compliance. Businesses and politics both attempt to benefit from fragmented structures of financial authorities. They look for ways and places that are more suitable for their goals. As a relatively innocent example, the race between cities in different countries to become "global financial centers" is largely a race to offer regulatory conditions that are more conducive to excessive risk taking for higher returns. It is like a race to provide easier regulatory arbitrage. There is still no globally binding regulatory framework (no "World Trade Organization" of finance), or even a mechanical framework for resolving legal conflicts. And this is not likely to change in years to come.

The second fundamental problem is the structural and conceptual fragmentation in regulation. Traditionally, regulation takes as a given the existing institutional structure and aims at ensuring its safety and integrity. This institution-oriented approach, however, has evolved into "regulatory blindness" because everything about finance has changed and the system has become more complex since the 1980s. The consequences of post-crisis regulation are in evidence. Everybody agreed that excessive debt (and the way it was structured) was the biggest root cause of the crisis and all agreed to reduce dependence on debt. Hence, new regulation aimed to deleverage bank balance sheets and bank credit was reduced as intended. However, this has shifted risk to non-bank firms doing what banks used to do before – lending, but this time under less or no supervision. Not only was the objective of reducing debt not achieved, but debt also increased faster and under riskier setups. Regulating banks alone did not do the job. A functional approach would aim at reducing debt by first defining the process of lending and borrowing as a function and then installing rules for fulfilling this function, regardless of who is lending or borrowing through any transactional channel whatever.

A second example of regulatory failure after 2008 is about the new stricter rules of CDS trading. As expected, the volume of CDS trading greatly decreased and standard CDS trading is limited to those exposed to the underlying loans. However, new structured products with new names such as "collateralized loan obligations" ("loan" replacing "debt") and "bespoke" default insurance contracts are becoming popular and they look very much like CDOs and CDSs with a small catch, in that they are not in the regulator's notebook. A functional approach to regulation would not fall into these traps. All quiet on this front too.

Correct and timely information is the single most valuable source of sense in finance. Markets cannot be sustainable and stable without asset valuations based on good information. Therefore, there are accounting and reporting regulations to ascertain the accuracy of information. Given the rules and standards of information construction and dissemination, regulation delegates the task of fact checking to audit firms and credit rating agencies. These firms play a critical role in financial intermediation because they intermediate between the sources and users of information. Despite their critical importance and frequent obvious failures, audit and rating services have not improved to any notable extent in the aftermath of the global crisis. They continue with, more or less, the same business models and a small number of firms maintain an oligopolistic control of the market. It has become like the "too-big-to-fail" problem in banking with similar potential for moral hazard.

There are two major accounting standards: GAAP (Generally Accepted Accounting Principles) used by American corporations and IFRS (International Financial Reporting Standards) by much of the rest of the world. The two sets of standards are not fully compatible and convergence attempts have not been very successful. This divergence may lead to ridiculous results in that a given asset or company can have a different reported value depending on the chosen standard. Such differences turn out to be vital in times of market turbulence, pre-IPO pricing and during M&A negotiations. Even within a given standard set, a vigilant financial manager can report different profits and asset values by a careful combination of footnotes and "exception" clauses, or picking the right audit firm. US GAAP and IFRS have both become patchworks of continual additions and revisions over the years. There are also fundamental conceptual problems such as misuses of "fair value" accounting that has plagued financial markets for decades. Behind the doors, even the most experienced IFRS and FASB (Financial Accounting Standards Boards) members do not trust corporate financial reporting at all. The industry is also closed to competition, where the "Big Four" companies (PwC, KPMG, Ernst and Young, Deloitte) audit more than 98% of FTSE 350 companies in the UK and S&P 500 companies in the US. They are powerful and difficult to supervise.

Credit rating agencies (CRA) have been hot topics of discussion and even subjects of Hollywood movies about the 2008 crisis. For several decades, CRAs have been criticized for optimistic ratings before debt crises and sudden downgrades afterwards. This pattern feeds euphoria and asset bubbles going into a crisis and faster contraction of liquidity after a crisis. As evidence, it is sufficient to remember how CDOs, Lehman Brothers and several soon-to-sink assets were rated highly only a few months before the crash. CRAs have failed in their duty to send warning signals to markets and have become more like "town criers" announcing bad news after it is too late. Clearly, their internal models have lost touch with reality and they can no longer assess risks properly. Reportedly, there are some improvements in rating models but they still have to be tested. The real problem is the industry convention where the entity being rated pays for the service. This is bad for many reasons but an alternative formula is yet to be designed. Furthermore, as in the audit industry, there is extreme market concentration with three large American CRAs (Standard & Poor's, Fitch and Moody's) accounting for more than 95% of all ratings. The SEC is reluctant to extend the list of rating agencies. We again have a case of a too-big-to-supervise and too-bossy-to-challenge industry.

On the policy-making front, central banks have come out of the last financial crisis significantly more powerful than ever before. Paul Tucker (2018, 3), deputy governor of the Bank of England during the crisis, explains in his recent book, *Unelected Power*, how central banks have emerged as a "new pillar of unelected power". In his book, *The Only Game in Town*, Mohammed El-Arian (2016) agrees with Tucker but also underscores the hazard of people perceiving central banks as more powerful than they can ever be. This is dangerous because, without due coordination with fiscal policy and other regulations, central banks will not be able to do much on their own in troubled times. It is dangerous also because an unelected power of money is more prone to political influence in good times and an easy scapegoat in bad times. It will not be good to face the next crisis with this background.

Despite a few weak voices of warning, central banks still refuse to accept that standard models of monetary policy are no longer sufficiently effective. They fail to take into account the redistribution channels of policy actions and also the distribution of debt capacity across income levels. It was clearly seen in the 2008 crisis that, after decades of financialization, asset bubbles in financial markets are "the tail that wags the dog" but monetary policy makers continue to believe that inflation is the single important signal of overheating in the economy. This belief may have some validity in economies with underdeveloped financial markets but certainly not in developed markets. In an economy such as the US or UK, where less than 10% of the population owns more than 90% of financial assets, increases in stock prices do not cause inflation. But when asset bubbles burst, the real economy enters a recession. Financial markets have not yet earned a central place in the models of central banks.

As they are not politically accountable, central banks can refuse to accept responsibility, offer public explanations, work with other regulators, and pay attention to business conduct. As a case of lack of coordination, how can we measure the actual result of stress tests or the sensibility of "living wills" when the realism of banks' financial reports is suspected even by the very writers of accounting standards? In a world where more than 90% of "money" is supplied by banks and the remainder by central banks, lack of coordination with fiscal authorities will result in ineffective monetary policy, at least insofar as the real economy is concerned. This is one face of central banks' lack of coherence with the real economy. Central banks are not as powerful as is thought because they do not work with other relevant players.

It may be true that agile and courageous actions of central banks – the Federal Reserve as the leader – prevented a bigger economic calamity in the aftermath of 2008. To prevent a global meltdown, more than $22 trillion of support was provided to the financial system. As a consequence of huge asset purchases by central banks from troubled banks and other indirect subsidies to financial markets, interest rates were drawn down to zero and even below zero. This was by far the biggest "quantitative easing" – a term made popular after the crisis – in known history, both in absolute and relative value. A deeper depression was avoided but, after a full decade, economic results are not even close to what standard macroeconomic models would predict, or hope for. A few indicators summarizing the state of the world in 2018 are given in Figure 2.25. Numbers are all but good.

Despite the most intensive expansionary policies in modern history, the performance of the world economy since 2008 has been relatively poor. Cumulative annual growth rates in global GDP from the depths of the crisis in 2008 to 2017 have been less than half of the growth rates between 2001 and 2008. This result is a surprise to all economists and it can only be explained in retrospect.

Despite the global will to deleverage after the crisis, debt has continued to increase. This increase has largely been in different segments of the market, in different regions and under new names. Lower interest rates have increased the demand for debt in general and, at the same time, a search for higher rates has increased the supply of debt to riskier borrowers. In economies with reduced bank credit, market-based credit such as corporate bonds has increased. An increasing percentage of bonds issued since 2009 have lower credit qualities (and hence higher yields). Shadow banks and many variants of non-bank lenders have increased their market shares. For example, a technology startup in the US has evolved into a financial firm called Quicken Loans to become the biggest home lender in the US. Whatever the details may be, the rise and rise of debt continues. In 2017, global debt as a proportion of GDP is fast approaching 350%, up from its previous peak of about 250% just before the crisis. Today the world is awash with debt.

The behavior of stock markets has also been striking. The total market value of the stocks in the S&P 500 index has quadrupled from a low of $6 trillion in 2009 to almost $25 trillion in 2018. Considering the brief time span, this is an unprecedented bull market. It is interesting to note that one-third of this increase is due to the top 10 highest valued technology firms such as Apple and Google. Apparently, cheap money has flooded stock markets. Relative to the performance of the real economy, stock market prices have increased beyond any rational valuation. Similar patterns can be seen in most of the stock markets in the world. This looks much like a big asset bubble, the work of quantitative easing.

The Case-Shiller home price index for the US shows a very similar pattern to debt and equity markets. From their lowest point in 2012 after a peak in 2007, nominal home prices in 2018 are higher than ever before. Subtracting inflation, real home prices are following suit and they are also headed for an all-time high very soon. The share of subprime mortgage lending in this increase may not be as high as it was before the 2008 crisis – and we do not know this for sure because the new players in home lending are not under close supervisory watch – but then prime mortgages may also default when used in excess. The pattern in Figure 2.25 shows a bubble or soon-to-be bubble in home prices.

Figure 2.25: State of the world in numbers

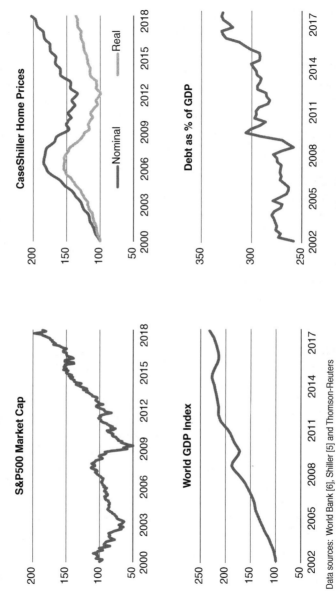

Data sources: World Bank [6], Shiller [5] and Thomson-Reuters

Slow growth in incomes, unleashed growth in debt, overpriced equity and housing markets do not portray a healthy world economy. To make matters worse, income inequality has reached worrisome levels and the rise of nationalist politics jeopardizes chances of global cooperation in case of trouble. The state of the world looks worse than the years before 2008. Extreme financialization is still everywhere and it does not take a genius to predict that the next financial crisis will be bigger and more destructive. It will also be more difficult to mitigate. History is repeating itself because we have not read it wisely.

Finance is based on trust. Addressing a Congressional hearing in 1912, legendary financier J.P. Morgan said: "character, before money or anything else. Money cannot buy it ... A man I do not trust could not get money from me on all the bonds in Christendom... I think that is the fundamental basis of business" (*Financial Times*, October 6, 2018). By the same token, a bank that people do not trust cannot get much of their money, or will be their first stop in a bank run. All events after 2008 wiped out most of what little was left of people's trust in the integrity of the financial industry and of "mainstream" politics' handling of finance. The common perception is that banks and bankers were saved at the expense of ordinary people's livelihoods. When it happens again, absence of trust will amplify a financial panic. Today, finance stands as a distrusted complex network of money flows and this should be a cause of deep concern. But that should not deter efforts to correct it. Using Keynes' famous words, "optimism is the highest level of intelligence", and it is time for a fresh approach to finance.

THREE

Good Finance

Collateral damage of the global financial crisis has gone much farther than a mere financial event. It has worsened income inequality, especially in the developed countries, and eroded people's trust in institutions and governments. This has given rise to an anomalous mix of populist and nationalist trends in societies and loss of faith in the merits of global policy cooperation and trade. Capitalism has come under scrutiny, both in open words and also in yet unspoken words, compromising the very ideal of free markets. This should not be allowed to take hold because free markets, despite all past abuses by bad people and firms, have produced tremendous gains in economic and social welfare since the 19th century. We cannot allow bad finance to hijack free markets. We cannot allow bad capitalism to drive out free markets.

The world needs a new paradigm of finance. Using terminology from political economics, we need to formulate a new "social contract" between policy makers, financial markets and people. This contract should remind us about the role of finance in our lives and redefine the real purposes of financial regulation and economic policy. The guiding principle is simple: a financial system is good for the society when it serves the basic functions outlined in the first paragraph of Chapter One – and does nothing more. It is bad when it produces complex inner structures to hinder these functions and turns into a positive-sum trade for itself by stealing from the main street. A bad businessman is bad but a bad financier is twice as bad.

Brief politics of household debt

This is not a book about the sociology or morality of debt in human societies. Several interesting new books deal with such issues to draw a different perspective to the 2008 financial crisis (Shiller, 2012; Plender, 2016; Bookstaber, 2017; Desai, 2017 and Tooze, 2018). However, in search for a solution to excessive debt, it may be useful to understand why people jump on credit whenever and however it is offered. Why do many people borrow more money than they can ever pay back? Why do banks and other creditors, with all their expertise in financial affairs, give out so much unpayable credit? Why do governments, whose duty is to protect their citizens and institutions, allow this to happen?

The answers can be found partly in human psychology and partly in misoriented politics. In our time, people look for happiness in material gains and hence a continual search for "better everything" in life – maybe until they get old enough to look back and see a mostly wasted effort. Such a lifestyle is possible only by spending more than one's income; that is, by borrowing. People like politicians who promise more spending for the people and by the people. And politicians who can actually deliver on their promises are re-elected. This, in turn, is possible by turning a blind eye to a financial system that has the technology and greed to produce ever-increasing levels of debt. Greed is for the interest charged on debt. More debt means more interest income for the creditor.

This chain of events continues until debt payments are due, but they cannot be paid back, ending with defaults and a financial crash. The sad finale is that the invoice for the crash is mailed back to the people, and not to the creditors. This is done to "save the financial system" and, after all, does not one have to pay one's debt? As a result, not only "borrowed wealth" is destroyed but also debt continues to rise. Household credit (home credit, student loans, credit cards and so on) are higher than household income in most of the developed countries and, as shown before, the difference has been on the rise since the 1970s. Most households in these countries spend their entire working ages struggling to pay back debt. Debt obligations may well continue into retirement (of course, if pensions are not wiped out by a crash by then). Such an economic landscape is not only socially immoral and unfair but also mathematically unsustainable. No specific side is to be blamed because all are responsible – unreflective people, conniving governments and greedy financiers. Households have to be "educated" in their dealing with debt, but there are difficulties.

Although banks are expected to channel household deposits into productive uses by firms, less than 15% of bank credit to non-financial debtors in the UK and US is credit to corporations, and the rest is credit to households to be spent on already existing goods, mostly homes. The purpose is not well served. Even then, curbing bank credit by stricter regulatory rules on bank leverage – as was done after 2008 – does not help reduce overall debt because then non-bank credit sources fill the gap – as was seen after 2010.

A further difficulty and moral problem with debt stems from the complexity of the financial system. Through a series of securitizations by intermediaries (remember CDOs), a person may be saving for retirement and simultaneously borrowing for consumption, where the original source of money is actually their own pension contributions! Legally, the person is indebted and has to pay the debt. A financial crisis can destroy pensions but does not erase debts. Clearly, the person would have been better off to have not saved or borrowed but instead had spent all income for current consumption and saved nothing for retirement. This is a moral dilemma because such debt is only imaginary and an artifact of financial complexity. Households may be financially illiterate and haphazard in their decisions but this does not change the fact that they are being treated unfairly by the system.

Since debt becomes a problem when it cannot be paid, public policy must be designed to prevent individuals from borrowing more than they can pay. Policy must also stop the financial system from producing unnecessary indebtedness as in the example of the previous paragraph. Regulating bank balance sheets alone cannot solve the problem. It never did and it never will. If excessive debt is not desired, then regulation must encompass all sources of credit, banks and non-banks alike. Defining creditworthiness as a function of income is not a difficult problem in financial engineering, and regulators can impose this function on all credit institutions. They should not be allowed to lend to people lacking adequate income to pay back. Technically, it is not hard to do.

Practical difficulty is the fact that curbing consumer debt is not a preferred choice for politicians. People will feel poorer as they cannot spend as much as when they could borrow beyond their limits. It will be unpopular and may be perceived as a breach of freedom of choice. (Such a perception is not well founded because freedom to borrow stupidly is not being limited. It can still be done outside of the financial system.) Assuming freedom does not give the right to damage oneself and indirectly damage others, this would be an excellent case for "nudging" because, with probability one, all will be better off in the long run. Once a societal equilibrium of beliefs and financial behavior is achieved, free markets will be stronger and more sustainable. Political "engineers" must be able to design an action plan that will not risk losing the next election – and they have succeeded in more difficult shifts of gear in the past. Crowds may behave irrationally against their own interests most of the time, but certainly not all of the time. Hence, an opportune time and condition can be found to mobilize politics. We just have to be careful not to be baffled by financial lobbies and turn banks into "central planning agencies of household debt".

Corporate choice between debt and equity

Corporate financing decisions about the use of debt and equity for investment in production shape the capital structure of the real economy. Over the last few decades, financialization is observable in corporate balance sheets too. In 2017, market values of corporate debt and equity were roughly equal at about $80 trillion each, which means that the financial sector (that is, debt) makes up about 50% of the assets of publicly listed companies. Estimates by economists at the New York Fed show that this ratio increases to 70% in the US when private companies are also taken into account. In other words, more than half of the total assets of non-financial companies are "owned" by creditors and other debt providers.

Percentage share of credit and credit-like securities in total corporate debt was about 94% in 2007 and the remaining 6% was made up of corporate bonds. Due to cutbacks in bank credit since, the share of bonds tripled to 18% by 2017. It is interesting to note further that 80% of all credit intermediation is done by shadow banks such as money market funds, insurance companies, broker-dealers, and more recently even private equity firms. Apparently, traditional commercial banks are not big players in the market for corporate debt. A new trend since the global crisis of 2008 has been the rising share of low-grade high-risk corporate debtors in the market. This trend is more pronounced in emerging markets like China. Firms in emerging markets borrow not only at high rates of interest but also often in foreign currencies, mostly US dollars.

It was mentioned before that annual new bond issues (the cumulative total of which is already less than one-fifth of total corporate debt) are four times all new equity issues by corporations. Corporations are heavily indebted and, if current conditions continue, they are likely to be more so in the future. Debt financing comes with the risk of financial distress, the risk of insolvency and eventually bankruptcy risk. If debt is denominated in a foreign currency, there is also additional currency risk because the foreign exchange value of the local currency can always depreciate. Some of these risks are manageable by conventional tools but most are not because they are systemic.

A mix of too much debt and too little equity in balance sheets seems to be the financial model of most corporations in the world. The question then is whether this is a reason for concern, or not. The theory of corporate finance as it is taught in schools today is not of much help in answering the question. The foundation of the theory can be credited to the seminal works of professors Franco Modigliani and Merton Miller in 1950s and 1960s. Their original theory ("M&M") was that, assuming a perfect market with no frictions and informational asymmetries, capital structure is irrelevant to firm value. Any mix of debt and equity is as good as any other (Modigliani and Miller 1958).

Over the years, many of the simplifying assumptions of the original M&M theory have been relaxed to make it more realistic, but its basic teaching has not changed much. Corporate management does not have to, and indeed cannot, do for shareholders what they can do for themselves. As a simple example, if a stock investor's preference of capital structure does not agree with that of any given company, they can set up a portfolio of companies with a resultant capital structure to their preference. In technical terms, market equilibrium will be at a point where corporate choices of capital mix are irrelevant to value. Capital structures of individual companies are irrelevant in a diversified portfolio of all companies because individual risks will be canceled out. This line of thinking may be perfect in theory but it does not have much practical validity in today's markets. Most ordinary people may also find these technical arguments absurd, and they are not too wrong.

The problem with the theory of corporate finance is that it is at best half a theory. It has a static one-step approach and fails to consider the consequences of its prescriptions. A case in point is the current state of the world. In a market where most companies are heavily debt-dependent and many are high-risk debtors, default by a small number of such companies cannot be assumed to have been simply diversified away in a large portfolio. Companies are systemically interconnected and there may be fast spillover effects. For instance, no economy or company with a business relationship with China can stay indifferent to the growing volume of junk corporate bonds and unregulated shadow banks in the country. China is big but only one of many similar cases. Just remember that the global meltdown in 2008 was triggered initially by a few defaults of really small high-risk mortgage debtors. Excessive debt and financial complexity have cast doubt on the teachings of current books on corporate finance. In all probability, Modigliani and Miller would have written differently had they lived today. Textbooks must be revised.

Choice between debt and equity must be re-examined with due attention to all we should have learned from past crises. It is a fundamental issue for the future welfare of societies. Global finance has arrived at a "T junction" with two alternative paths forward. One path is continuing as before with constantly rising levels of debt. This is tantamount to acceptance of increasing frequency and magnitude of financial crises, low economic growth, high unemployment and further distortion in income inequality. The other path is realizing that excessive debt is the root of all financial evil and duly reforming the discipline of finance to serve society better.

Historically, the words "debt", "trespass" and "sin" have been synonyms in popular prayers. Indeed, in the old Aramaic language, the word for "debt" and the word for "sin" are the same.[21] Polonius in Shakespeare's *Hamlet* advises his son: "Neither a borrower nor a lender be / for loan oft loses both itself and friend / and borrowing dulls the edge of husbandry" (Act 1, scene 3, 75–77). In past societies, debt was not a desirable thing to have. In modern societies, if a moral tag is to be attached to debt, it would refer to excessive debt as a "societal sin" when improbability of repayment is known a priori. Such creditors and debtors are both harming the society.

In contrast, the word "equity" refers to a desirable property to have. The word comes from old English *equite*, from old French *équité*, and from Latin *aequitas*. Its dictionary meaning is the quality of being fair and just. In law, it is the principle of justice which is used in cases where laws are insufficient, and it implies courage and sportsmanship. Hence, it must be no coincidence that a corporation's shares of ownership, which carry no guaranteed profit like fixed interest, are also called equity. Corporate equity comes with equitable sharing of profits and risks. In market-based economies, courage to do business in a world of uncertainties is the only real source of economic progress and equity is the only financial contract that can handle such entrepreneurial courage.

Companies cease to exist either because they default on debt or because they have a bad business idea (that is, people do not purchase their products). All of the startup companies that fail early, fail because of a bad business idea. Most of the "seasoned" companies that fail eventually, fail because of inability to pay their debt. Excessive debt is the single most observed reason for business failure.

If a company with a bad business idea and no debt goes out of business, it will be a good thing because valuable resources that are freed up can be better utilized elsewhere. But if a company which has a good business idea but cannot service its debt goes out of business, it will be a bad thing because valuable resources are then often wasted. Short of bankruptcy, in economic slowdowns heavily indebted companies turn into "debt payment machines", drown in high-risk short-term projects leading to destruction of long-term value. Moreover, urgency of payments leaves no time to behave in a socially responsible manner. These are the real social costs of too much debt.

Debt is not capital, it is only borrowed money that has to be paid back no matter what. But equity is genuine capital. Remember a total global debt of almost $300 trillion and a notional value of more than $500 trillion in interest rate derivatives, most of them designed to manage the risks of this very debt. Preference for debt over equity has produced a need to manage artificially instigated financial risks and this effort, in turn, has crowded out genuine entrepreneurial courage. Managers and owners of companies struggling with debt payments can lose their entrepreneurial spirit very easily. Equity financing is in decline in most advanced economies. Excessive corporate debt is hijacking valuable sources of productive capital. It is like making trouble first and then trying to mitigate it.

Except for underdeveloped poor countries, all of the economies in the world are dominated by private sector companies. Therefore, if companies do well, then the economy grows and more people are employed, and vice versa. Economic growth in advanced countries between the Second World War and the 1980s has been financed largely by public equity, as in the US, and equity-like long-term project-finance credit, as in Germany. Historically, there is no country and no major company that has been able to achieve sustainable long-term growth based only on bank credit. Recent economic instability in some emerging countries is largely due to excess debt in general and excess debt in foreign currencies in particular. Unless they can reduce dependence on debt and broaden their countries' equity base, their economies will continue on a bumpy path with a danger of sudden stops at any time.

Equity is not only a desirable type of financial contract but is also the most profitable investment by a wide margin. With rare exceptions, the most valuable companies in the world are publicly held companies. The wealth of the world's richest people is largely made up of their equity holdings. *Forbes* magazine's annual lists of billionaires provide ample evidence of this (Forbes, 2018). Figure 3.1 illustrates the long-term performance of stocks, bonds and bills in the US since 1927. For the period from 1927 to 2017, the graphs show the value of $100 invested in a broad-based portfolio of stocks, in 10-year Treasury bonds and in short-term Treasury bills, where interim cash flows (dividends on stocks and coupon payments on bonds) are reinvested in the same vehicle. Numbers are nominal values before taxes.

In the 90 years since 1927, $100 invested in US equities has phenomenally grown to about $400,000, which is not even comparable with returns on bonds and bills. The period notably includes both the Great Depression of 1929 and the global crisis of 2008. During the period, after adjusting for taxes and inflation, the real geometric mean rate of return on stocks has been 6% per year and the real rate of interest has been 1% per year. Equity investment has been so much more profitable. It is no wonder that the authors of the Credit Suisse's Yearbook had titled their previous book *Triumph of the Optimists* (Dimson et al, 2002). Courage to invest and patience to wait for results

Figure 3.1: Long-term performance of stocks and bonds

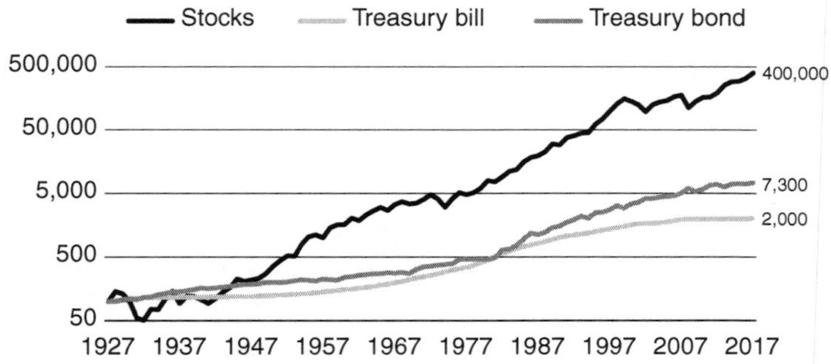

Source: Dimson et al (2017)

pay handsomely in the long run. This is how market-based economies advance. Consequently, if stocks are so profitable for investors, then companies should have no difficulty in raising equity capital. There should not be a problem of demand. But the financial system today does not seem to allow that to happen. Debt has been made easier to find, and it has been continuously fed into the economy. This is a malfunction in the system and it has to be corrected. Valuable resources are being wasted because debt cannot be a surrogate for equity by any means.

Currently, tax codes in most countries favor debt issuance over equity financing. In OECD countries, corporations enjoy an average of 10% in tax savings when they use interest-bearing debt instead of equity. It is common knowledge that mere tax deductibility of interest payments is often the only motivation to issue debt. This is a moral hazard because the real consequences of borrowing are largely disregarded. First of all, tax codes and regulations must be changed to level the playing field between debt and equity. Tax treatment of dividends must be the same as that of interest payments, both as taxable income and as a tax-deductible expense. Budget structures of governments may not be the same in all countries and different solutions may be necessary. Whatever country-specific cases may be, tax rules about dividends and interest income must be equitable.

Another major obstacle to equity financing is commercial codes and securities regulation. In almost all jurisdictions, the regulatory burden on public equity offerings is many times heavier than that on public offerings of debt securities. This burden covers the full range of regulations including rules of public disclosure, corporate governance, supervisory oversight and market trading. For example, regulation demands a detailed (but often with inadequate valuable information) prospectus from companies in initial public offerings of equity shares, but in public offerings of corporate bonds either a very short prospectus, or none, is required. A company that has $100 million worth of listed shares has to comply with all of the relevant securities regulations whereas a company with $100 billion of publicly floated bonds does not have to comply with most of them. Of course, equity and bonds are not the same animals and they will be treated differently. But it is still difficult to explain why holders of $100 billion worth of bonds should not have a right to know about the company's handling of corporate governance and engage as stakeholders. It is also hard to justify why regulators enforce minimum supervision on private companies with huge volumes of publicly traded bonds.

Naturally, since equity represents ownership and debt does not, regulation of equity securities requires more care and detail than that of debt securities. However, this fact has to be read wisely because when the dose of regulatory difference is exaggerated, the risk of "regulatory cronyism" arises. For issuers of bonds to the public, lack of sufficient regulatory oversight may result in careless management of risks of debt because there will not be a coherent group of stakeholders demanding information and accountability. This also implies a moral hazard in optimizing corporate capital structures, and excessive debt will again prevail.

Burdensome regulation of equity securities coupled with a one-size-fits-all approach makes it very difficult for small, growing companies to access public markets. This issue has been on the agenda of policy makers and regulators for years but no satisfactory solution is yet in sight. Anyone who has been a regulator, or worked with regulators, knows that regulators simply do not like small companies. They do not like them because they presume that smaller companies come with higher probabilities of failure and no bureaucrat wants to take that risk. And their dislike of small companies is supposedly justified by their mandate of investor protection. This is an absurd argument because keeping growth companies out of the public markets pushes them towards private debt, which further increases their already "high probability" of failure. What if a growth company has a very bright business idea and is a genuine candidate for being a superstar of the future? Growth companies cannot be tomorrow's Apple or Microsoft if they are blocked out from public equity markets. Apple and Microsoft did not grow their businesses by borrowing from banks. They enjoyed the blessings of equity markets of their earlier times.

As a matter of fact, investors are better protected when law makers and regulators can make a wiser analysis of real growth dynamics. Investors are actually disserved when entrepreneurial courage is not applauded. After all, investor protection can be maximized by shutting down all markets! Need for investor protection should not be an excuse for preventing growth companies' access to public equity markets. Regulators must be sympathetic to small companies.

Another structural obstacle to equity financing is the new business model of stock exchanges. The turn of the century witnessed several mergers and acquisitions among stock exchanges and most have transformed into for-profit corporations listed in one of their own subsidiary exchanges. The basic function of a stock exchange is to serve as a public platform where companies can obtain equity capital via primary market offerings, followed by efficient production of information for value discovery and ownership engagement via secondary market trading. By and large, this function is no longer served. Today, stock exchanges focus more on other revenue sources such as derivatives trading, electronic funds trading, algorithmic trading and data sales. In order to generate aimless liquidity, which has no or very little relevance for value discovery, trading has been surrendered to speedy robots trading in nanoseconds. Genuine equity trading has been put on the backburner. The number of listed companies and the number of IPOs have declined considerably.

With doors closed to small, growing companies, stock trading in exchanges is now mostly confined to the shares of the top 5% most traded companies, which also make up more than half of total market capitalization. New small companies cannot enter and previously listed small companies are neglected on the trading platform. This is not why stock exchanges exist and, in their current models of business, they are of little relevance for the real economy. For fear of their company turning into a trading toy of algorithmic games, no entrepreneur in their right mind will look for equity financing in today's stock exchanges. And they do not. This is unfortunate but it can be corrected very easily.

Securities and exchange regulators can define two alternative models of exchanges. The first model is a stock exchange which focuses on public trading of equities, equity-linked instruments and corporate bonds only. An immediate example is the good old New York Stock Exchange, fully committed to serving the basic economic functions of a stock exchange but now empowered with all the new technologies. The second model can be an exchange (but not called "stock exchange") doing everything current exchanges can do but without basic equity trading. Regulation must be carefully designed to make sure that the second model does not crowd out the first one. Variants of this proposal may also be imagined but, in any case, we need to win back useful stock exchanges primarily focused on serving their fundamental economic functions.

The growing spiral of debt

A final digression on debt may be appropriate to set the stage for a discussion of policy making and regulation in finance. The first step is to realize that most of what we call "money" is actually *credit* created in the financial system. Only a small portion of the money supply is physical banknotes printed by governments (so-called "legal tender"). Imagine a primitive scenario of a new economy with a new bank welcoming its first deposit of $100 in banknotes and then extending its first credit of $100. When the borrower spends this amount, it is channeled back into the bank increasing total deposits to $200. Now the bank can now give out an additional $100 credit, increasing total credits to $200, and so on. If this deposit-to-credit-to-deposit chain process is repeated 10 times, the result will be total deposits of $1,100 and total credit of $1,000 (assuming the bank keeps $100 of cash as reserves). The amount of money in the economy is $1,100 composed of $100 of physical banknotes ("central bank money") and $1,000 of credit ("bank money"). Also note that total amount of spending during the process was also equal to $1,100.

In reality, it is estimated that the total amount of money in the world is the equivalent of about $95 trillion and less than $7 trillion of this is printed money in various currencies. The remainder is credit, which is necessarily measured in units of some legal tender.[22] Given this picture, it is accurate to say that world business and commerce run on "credit money" (not on banknotes or coins or some physical commodity). This monetary function is indeed why banks are posed as too important to fail, both politically and legally. Under this design, monetary expansion is mostly credit expansion and bank credit is people's debt. Ray Dalio (2018), successful financier and thinker, has developed an intuitive and knowledgeable presentation of "credit cycles". Economies ride on credit cycles.

As an accounting identity, a person's spending is equal to their total income plus credit. Spending can be on current consumption as well as on real (e.g. houses) and financial assets (e.g. stocks, pensions). Someone's credit limit depends on their creditworthiness, which in turn depends on their income level and also on the value of collateral they can provide to the creditor. Thus, when income rises, credit also rises and this results in more spending. Since one person's spending is another person's income, more spending increases incomes and values of assets. As incomes and asset values increase, supply of credit further increases, triggering more spending. Economic expansion continues to a point where spending starts to exceed the quantity of goods and assets available, which then causes inflation. To curb inflation, central banks respond by hiking interest rates, which then makes credit more costly and hence less available. This triggers a chain of events: reduced spending, reduced incomes and depressed asset values. A recession starts and defaults on credit start to show up. Then central banks change gear and decrease the rate of interest. This makes available more credit and starts a new upswing of another cycle.

Credit expansion in a new upswing will be bigger than that in the previous cycle because not only is new credit needed for new spending but also debts accumulated from the previous economic boom will not have been fully paid back. As a result, the bottom of each new cycle will be higher than the bottom of the previous cycle. In the long run, bottom–line credit growth continues for years until debt service becomes impossible. This is just another face of financialization happening faster than real economic growth and the story ends with a catastrophe like the 2008 crisis. And all of the global aftershocks and social harm continue for years.

Careful thinking reveals two basic problems in the current financial architecture producing credit and business cycles. The first is that credit expands faster than income during economic booms but it also contracts less than income during economic downturns. In the long run, credit always rises faster than income until a big crash in markets. The catch is that it is the volume of credit that determines the ups and downs in spending and not the changes in real productivity. This problem is that credit cycles are rooted in the center of all parametric models of standard monetary policy.

The second problem is conceptually more foundational and thus more difficult to tackle. Growth in income is equal to the sum of inflation and productivity growth. Productivity is the amount of goods and services produced per unit of resource. In the long run, it is the only genuine measure of economic welfare. Cost of credit (rate of interest) is the sum of inflation, the real rate of interest and risk premium. In credit models, risk premium is a compensation for the risk of default by the debtor and it is assessed by the creditor considering the unique risk of a given debtor and also overall risks in credit markets. When the economic cycle is up, risk premia are low. In downturns, for fear of increasing defaults, risk premia are set higher and interest rates go up. This pattern of behavior by creditors does not match the needs of debtors but it is normal because credit is their way of making money and it is not the creditors' job to manage the real economy. But then, in the long run, this makes the average rate of interest higher than the average rate of growth in income, and the net gains remain with the creditors. This is a systematic problem.

History reminds us of a mathematical fact about credit cycles: regardless of the ratio of credit to income, eventual default by debtors is inevitable when interest rates are higher than the growth rate in income. The ratio of credit to income only determines how soon and how deep the defaults will be. The higher this ratio is, the sooner and the more damaging the defaults will be. Such endings are called financial crises or crashes. Too much debt is bad but it gets worse when the cost of debt is higher than the rate of growth in economic productivity in the long run.

For economic growth, we do not have to live with credit cycles if monetary policy and people's attitude towards consumption can be transformed. An immediate prescription for consumers is not to let debt rise faster than income and not to be a net borrower to spend on consumption alone. If your income is not high enough, do not use bank credit (for example credit card) to buy a new 50-inch TV set, which is a zero productivity investment. Similarly, companies should not borrow to invest unless the expected rate of return on the investment is comfortably higher than the cost of debt. In today's societies, as long as credit is so abundantly available and a live-the-day-forget-tomorrow attitude is so deeply rooted, such prescriptions cannot go further than wishful thinking.

However, there are several steps societies can take to break the dependence on credit cycles. First, we have to challenge the whole concept and design of debt as a financial instrument. This starts with realizing that any financial contract with unfair terms of sharing risks and returns between two parties is bound to end with the eventual default of either side. Most modern debt and debt-based contracts are so, and this is probably what is meant by the popular term "the dark side of debt". Even in the least unfair cases, there are informational asymmetries between professional creditors and financially illiterate debtors. Imagine a case of a simple credit contract where the debtor pledges collateral to the creditor and naturally accepts the obligation of orderly repayment of principal plus some interest. In most countries, the market value of acceptable collateral is required to be much greater than the expected value of the total debt obligation. It is clear that most of the risk stays with the debtor and most of the expected return accrues to the creditor. The creditor can also buy insurance against the debtor's default and reflect the cost of insurance in the interest rate. It is at this point that any "human" relation between the creditor and the debtor ceases to exist and the creditor is now indifferent to the default of the debtor. When similar contracts become market-wide practice, defaults and economic recessions are guaranteed. All past crises, and certainly the most recent crisis, have proven this fact.

An extreme case of unfair financial contracts under law is the case of Spain. If a Spaniard defaults on their mortgage payments and the bank forecloses the house, the debtor continues to be fully liable for the full principal! This is based on a very old law. After the Spanish housing bubble in 2000s ended with widespread defaults causing a serious recession, this harsh law was widely learned about and protested against. Today, the law remains unchanged and the argument is that such a law is needed to protect the banking industry and strong banks are needed for economic recovery. But it did not work. Spain is still in a recession and Spanish banks are in a worse shape now than before. As extreme as it may be, the Spanish story shows the true dark side of debt. There is a general need to reassess the founding concepts of current commercial and bankruptcy laws in light of the new highly financialized world – a new task for academics and practicers of law.

Legal issues aside, and as explained above, the issue is that credit cycles move in opposition to "interest rate cycles" and, in contrast to both, real income and productivity growth display stable trends over time. This mismatch between the rate of income growth and the cost of debt is the major cause of defaults and of practical difficulties in management of bond portfolios. To tackle these problems, Robert Shiller (2012) proposes a debt instrument called "GDP-linked bonds" for governments. The interest rate on these bonds is tied to changes in the GDP of the issuing country. In economic booms these bonds yield higher rates and in economic downturns they yield less. This setup would not only prevent sovereign defaults but also provide a higher average rate of return for their investors. If it were not for fear of defaults, who would not want to make money on the very high growth rates in emerging economies over the past few decades? No government wants to default and nobody wants governments to default or fall into budget problems. The proposal is very wise.

Shiller's vision can be carried forward to corporate debt and even household debt, including personal debt such as student loans. A model of income-linked credit can be beneficial for these private markets for the same reasons GDP-linked bonds are good for sovereigns. Such an understanding would solve most of the inherent problems of debt and credit. First of all, defaults would be minimized, which is good for both debtors and creditors. This implies a fair sharing of returns and risks. It may sound counterintuitive at first but a careful analysis shows that income-linked credit is actually more profitable for the creditors. Costs of write-offs and costs of risk management will be largely eliminated. Most importantly, in order to earn more, creditors will search for corporations and households which have higher expected rates of growth in income and productivity. This is good for overall economic welfare as well because resources will then be allocated to more productive uses. Moreover, costs of cleanup after a crisis will be reduced and tax payers will be freed from having to pay for costly bailouts.

It may take a long while for financial innovations to take hold in markets. The idea of income-linked debt may seem strange in today's financial markets but it only takes one successful application to seed the model. If it is good, it must be doable. Financial engineers, who have been so talented in designing more complex "toxic" instruments, should be able to design this model without much difficulty. Of course, it will help if the first implementation of the model comes from a major government and from a major global financial institution.

So far, we have been beating up debt. However, this should not mean that all debt is bad. Access to credit is a necessity for companies and households and, if properly used, debt is a convenient tool for short-term management of budgets and as a buffer against short-term surprises. The important point here is that excessive debt and especially badly designed debt contracts are dangerous and must be avoided. The path to good finance first passes through reducing society's dependence on harmful types of debt. Laws and regulations must be revised and managers of our money must be educated better.

Financial regulation and banking

The 2008 crisis was the biggest financial crisis in recorded history and its impact on the world order is to be lived for many years yet to come. The events that led to the crisis did not happen overnight. Since the early 1990s, global integration of financial markets made possible large capital flows across borders and liquidity was abundant all over the world. Poorly designed monetary policies were applauded for keeping interest rate low and inflation under control. This triggered an unprecedented explosion of debt and toxic derivatives in volumes of hundreds of trillions. An excessive appetite for risk, fraud, disregard for good governance and deception of ordinary investors became widespread. Such market processes take years to evolve, and they take place under the close watch of financial regulators and central banks. The 2008 crisis was neither a "perfect storm" nor a "notably rare exception". It was a case of colossal failure of financial regulation and macroeconomic models.

In its current format, financial regulation follows problems and crises – they deal with what has happened and not with what might happen. Historically, most new rules and regulations are written to make sure that *known* problems do not repeat themselves. This approach is incomplete because rules are easily overcome by those who have the ingenuity, especially in today's markets opaqued by extreme complexity and fast change. It also triggers a moral hazard risk, where regulators and policy makers tend to defend the status quo by hiding behind the excuse of not having the necessary toolkits to fight crises. Regulators are not interested in "preventive medicine" and they are continually occupied with "local surgery" after the disease has already advanced.

The preamble of the Dodd–Frank Act of 2010 reads:

> An Act: To promote the financial stability of the United States by improving accountability and transparency in the financial system, to end too big to fail, to protect the American taxpayer by ending bailouts, to protect consumers from abusive financial services practices, and for other purposes.

The full text of this most comprehensive act as a response to the 2008 crisis is more than 800 pages. In addition to several wishes for moral behavior (which is a good thing in principle), it only aims at correcting regulatory and policy mistakes that were made after the crisis. By and large, it does not address most of the fundamental causes of crises.

After having worked with regulators from many different countries and as a former securities regulator, personal experience shows that the overwhelming majority of financial regulators are highly talented and honest people devoted to public service. But then, throughout the rise of modern finance since 1980s, they have failed terribly to protect society from the harm of bad finance. Without any malice whatsoever, their actions and inactions have exacerbated financial crises. So there must be a problem with the system of regulation, not with regulators as humans. It has to be fixed.

Drowning in the complexity and size of finance, financial regulators are blinded by a superficial and flawed understanding of the meaning of free markets. By virtue of their job, regulators have to be in continuous and close contact with the industry. They live and work with industry professionals, who have impressive credentials and "selling" skills – and are better paid than public servants. Regulators are trained not to give in to the opinions of the industry and they do not. The problem is that they genuinely *believe* in most of those opinions simply because they are products of free markets! In the meantime, however, they may forget their foremost duty of protecting society's interest. Free markets will not allow bad products to sell but bad products backed by regulatory approval will sell. Regulatory approvals and exemptions facilitate undue market acceptance. Such outcomes are surely not what regulators intend but there is still an obvious negligence of duty.

An unintended result of "regulator-industry intimacy" is what some describe as the "revolving doors of finance", and it forces the limits of ethics and integrity. Too many people change jobs back and forth between regulatory agencies and financial institutions. And many regulators start working for finance companies after leaving public office. Goldman Sachs, Citigroup and a few other too-big-to-fail banks emerge as favorite choices for departing senior regulators. It is natural human psychology to "go easy" on friends and ex-colleagues. This relationship puts a final icing on the cake called "financial lobby", and the power of finance in lobbying politicians is common knowledge. This may be good for the industry but surely not for the society at large.

All of this evinces an obvious lack of proper governance in the regulatory architecture. Good governance of regulatory agencies starts with a clear comprehension of why they exist, of their objectives, and how they will achieve those objectives. If the economic function of financial markets is to meet the needs of savers (owners of capital) and companies (users of capital), then financial regulation exists to ascertain that this function is well served – well served for savers and companies, period.

Today, regulation is more institution-oriented than function-oriented. Mottos like "market integrity" and "safety of banks" are common in the regulator's rule books. Any innovation – harmful and useful alike – may be acceptable as long as it does not damage market integrity and the safety of banks. And innovations are almost always the ideas of high-level intellectuals and subsequent designs by the industry. Smartly designed financial products can be convincingly presented as enhancing market integrity and the safety of banks. This results in "intellectual capture of the industry" and "regulatory capture by the industry" as explained above. In the process, it gets forgotten whether there is any benefit for savers and companies, and whether the industry is behaving with integrity. A new product that serves only the interests of the financial firms but has no apparent social benefit should not be encouraged.

In all fairness, it would be wrong to imply that the financial sector is fully crowded by greedy and relentless people. Such rotten apples are only a few, but still enough to erode people's trust in the system. Revising Gordon Gekko's famous words in the movie *Wall Street*: "greed is good … [if and only if it promotes not only individually beneficial but also socially good innovation]". Finance is not like any other kind of business; it touches all the people. Financial regulation should guide Gekko to use his talents towards such innovations. It is a market-based economy and it is okay if Gekko makes a lot of money. But it is the regulator's duty to make sure that he does not do so using only other people's money. Otherwise, the whole point is lost.

Lack of functional focus also results in superfluous regulation that does not serve even its own purpose. For example, Basel III rules were effective in reducing bank credit but did not even come close to reducing aggregate credit. Non-bank credit quickly filled in the gap and even went further. The purpose was to deleverage the economy but only bank balance sheets were deleveraged. A functional approach would aim at reducing credit regardless of its origin. Selective focus on the safety of banks hindered the intended outcome. Both in banking regulation and securities regulation, there are many similar cases of failure.

In order to install a proper governance structure for financial regulation, the first step is to unite banking and securities regulation under a single governing authority, and simultaneously reduce the amount of regulation. In today's complex industry structure with systemic interconnections all over the world, fragmented and complex regulation with zillions of rules does not and cannot serve any good. It can only cause instability, complexity and all the undesirable results mentioned throughout the book. The proposed body can organize in terms of functions such as credit origination, securities issuance, exchange trading and the like. The guiding principle must not be "who can do what and how?", as today, but instead "what can be done and how?" We need simple regulation locked onto socially beneficial targets. Names of institutions, instruments and procedures may be left to the details of secondary regulations.

Function-based regulation must start by first accepting that finance is not about finance only. A model of good regulation considers not only financial metrics but also environmental, social and governance issues. Finance is about managing all of financial, human, physical and ethical capital. It is about not only prudence and compliance but also integrity. Integrity and care for reputation must be incentivized by regulation, directly or indirectly. Compliance with laws and regulations does not necessarily produce a "good" person out of a "bad" person. Therefore, regulation should not allow investment in reputation to go unnoticed and unrewarded. Of course, all of these wishes cannot be translated into lists of written rules. The message here is that the mindset of regulators and law makers must work as such.

Good corporate governance (both for market participants and also for regulators themselves) should be at the core of any regulatory framework. Without good corporate governance, investor trust cannot be regained, and without investor trust, equity and bond markets cannot fulfill their fundamental functions. In the absence of functional public markets, domestic economies and global economic balances may veer in undesirable directions and economic growth cannot be sustainable.

Financial regulation should favor long-termism against short-termism. This calls for effective stakeholder engagement for good corporate governance and accepting that supervisors cannot do what stakeholders should be doing for themselves. Most importantly, pension funds, insurance funds and mutual funds should not be "pushed" to be short-termist by regulatory calls for short-term performance reports. On the contrary, regulation of institutional investors should provide incentives in favor of long-term performance. In particular, pension funds and wealth funds should comply with those rules of corporate governance that are in line with long-term value generation. Even if short-termism by some financial players is here to stay, this should not necessarily translate into short-termism by corporate management and boards. This can easily be achieved by regulatory rules allowing only "long-term" shareholders to vote in annual meetings. "Transient visiting investors" and HFT traders are not interested in ownership and they should not have voting rights. Tourists cannot vote in public elections and gamblers do not run the casino. By the same token, executive bonuses should be based only on long-term economic value added, not on quarterly or annual results. Prioritizing long-term performance and reward will eliminate most of the misbehavior that led to the crisis.

Regulation should enhance small companies' access to market-based financing and ensure equitable financial inclusion of people at all levels of income. This is a necessary condition for the sustainability of free markets. Free markets are possible if and only if there is good public governance, implying equitable and fair treatment of all players. Listing requirements and trading rules can be adjusted to fairly accommodate companies of all sizes and age.

A fundamental overhaul in monetary policy making is also needed. Standard models do not work as desired. Much can be said to reform monetary policy. Central banking should be repositioned to pay due attention to other public policies and financial regulation. Monetary policy must be reformulated to consider the inner structures of the real economy, especially the distributional channels of credit. Models of monetary policy by central banks and models of fiscal policy by treasuries must work in harmony. There seems to be a lot of homework for economists.

We must also recognize that most relations in today's markets are systemic and interconnected. New technologies may be harnessed to observe and supervise financial flows across the globe. Quoting Andy Haldane (2014, 7) of the Bank of England:

> I have a dream. It is futuristic, but realistic. It involves a Star Trek chair and a bank of monitors. It would involve tracking the global flow of funds in close to real time (from a Star Trek chair using a bank of monitors), in much the same way as happens with global weather systems and global internet traffic. Its centerpiece would be a global map of financial flows, charting spill-overs and correlations. (Maxwell Fry Annual Global Finance Lecture 2014)

Considering recent advances in information technologies, this is not an unrealistic expectation today and deserves serious attention.

Assuming all of the above are done, there is still a big fundamental challenge. No matter how financial regulation is reformed and how monetary policy is reformulated, banks will continue to occupy the core of the whole financial system. Under the current paradigm, banks are the major suppliers of money (or credit) and they are also the central intermediary of all monetary transactions with real and financial assets. They are the single most powerful component simply because money and credit are supplied by banks. This makes them practically more powerful than central banks. But then they are also the biggest source of risk in the system and they have much to be blamed for in most of the financial crises. Banks are not elected by popular vote and they are not meant to be public servants but they are the makers of money. This is how financial history has evolved.

After the 2008 crisis, politicians and regulators saved the banks but people never forgave them. This feeling is deeply rooted and it will not go away anytime soon. The immorality and fallacy of the concept "too-big-to-fail" was probably the worst thing to come out of the crisis. People's trust has to be won back. In the 1990s, when the internet was still very new, Bill Gates of Microsoft had famously voiced a vision: "We need banking, but we don't need banks" (Amberber, 2015). We may need most of the things done by Goldman Sachs and Deutsche Bank but we do not need Goldman Sachs and Deutsche Bank to do them for us. At the time, Gates' vision may have been taken as mere science fiction but today it is well worth pondering on. In light of all the flaws in the global financial system, we must reassess the vital role banks play. Maybe it is time to question why banks should exist.

In implementation, the most difficult and time-consuming problem facing public policy makers and financial regulators will be redefining the whole concept of financial regulation. The current practice of regulation is heavily based on the presence of intermediaries (banks, exchanges, brokers, audit firms, investment funds, clearing houses, insurance companies, trade repositories and so on) and much of regulation is done by regulating the intermediaries. For regulators, intermediaries are the sources of data about market activity and investor behavior. Historically, the current financial system has evolved as such. However, complexity of the intermediation business is a major problem of finance and there is clear need to remove all or some of these intermediaries. The big question is then how regulation will redefine and reshape its traditional intermediary–dependent model in the new financial markets without intermediaries. In this regard, new technologies such as blockchains may be considered as both a market structure and also a regulatory/supervisory platform. Regulators should pay attention to new technologies.

Finally, in today's interconnected world, national success stories alone will not suffice to get the desired results. Regulatory arbitrage across jurisdictions and tendencies by some countries to be free-riders will weaken the effectiveness of domestic regulations. Global coordination and harmony are needed. Today, the composition of international standard setters (such as the Financial Stability Board of the G20, Basel Committee on Banking Supervision, International Organization of Securities Commissions and Committee on Payment and Settlement Systems) do not fairly represent the distribution of wealth across advanced, emerging and developing economies and hence fail to consider the changing gravity of economic power. Decision-making procedures in these institutions must be properly designed to achieve global compliance. All countries should involve, contribute and comply.

Known risks and new uncertainties

As finance has become bigger and more complex, regulation has followed suit. This in turn has increased the importance of risk management and regulatory compliance. Today, companies employ teams of risk managers and compliance experts. Both functions have become areas of specialization and they comprise a big but unnamed industry. For people with entrepreneurial drives, risk and compliance people are often irritating because their most popular word is "no" and their favorite phrase is "I do not endorse it, do it at your own peril". In troubled times, their importance and power within the organization increase and, since the 1990s, troubled times seem never to end in the financial industry.

It is hard to understate the importance of managing financial risk and of compliance with laws and regulations. The amount of valuable resources allocated to risk management and compliance is naturally proportional to the degree of complexity in the underlying environment. And the final success of these activities is inversely related to the same degree of complexity. Then, failures in risk management, or difficulty in mitigating certain risks, are more probable in more complex settings. Were the underlying structure less complex, there would not be a need to invest so much in risk management and failures would be fewer. There is a dilemma and the only way to resolve it is to make the financial industry less complex. It is absurd to spend valuable resources on managing the risks *manufactured* by self-inflicted complexity. Moreover, management of self-inflicted risks is doomed to failure because motivation to make money from complexity – which requires excessive risk taking – can easily overcome the efforts of risk managers to prevent it. Risk managers are employed by risk takers.

In addition to the above structural problem, widely used models of risk assessment and management are largely mathematical, computable and algorithmic. They are sophisticated models demanding in-depth advanced analytical knowledge. However, events since the turn of the century have shown that they are not as useful as expected. Until the 2008 crisis, AIG was known to have the best models of risk management in basic insurance business and indeed they did. Overconfidence in the success of its existing models motivated the company to sell credit default insurance (CDSs) because the blind presumption was that insurance is insurance. Then they failed terribly and were bailed out by the US government. Such errors of judgment are by no means limited to AIG. It is an industry-wide problem.

Mathematical models of risk management are based on unrealistic assumptions about the underlying stochastic structures in markets and often miss sudden structural changes. Overreliance on such models and failure to recognize their limitations define a moral hazard case whereby companies get caught unprepared in crisis times. Management of financial risks is a necessity but it must be recognized that good-time correlations may be very different from bad-time correlations, and that there is no one good model of risk, which will always stay good. The risk of risk management must be seriously recognized.

Compared to known financial risks (market risk, credit risk and so on), new sources of uncertainty are more dangerous in the long run and they are often mathematically unmeasurable. To name a few, geopolitical conflicts, political violence, humanitarian crises, trade disputes, environmental catastrophes, technological disruptions and the yet undefined rule of law and rule of ethics in big data are new sources of risk and uncertainty. Failure to recognize these new sources of uncertainty and overreliance on existing mathematical models imply a new layer in risk of risk management. The distinction between mathematically modelable risks and mathematically unmeasurable uncertainties must be made clear and a new approach to risk management must be developed. Some risks are known (or knowable) and some are unknown (or unknowable). Thanks to technology and global interconnectedness, the modern-day problem is that new types of risk and uncertainty do not evolve slowly. They arrive suddenly. Mathematics and computing power may not be sufficient to manage these, and proper "risk observatories" have to be developed. The operating model of risk observatories must be based on the investment strategies of prudent and patient businessmen like Warren Buffett and Ray Dalio, and not on the modeling talents of financial mathematicians.

Financial education and literacy

After the 2008 crisis, there were several attempts, both by governments and by NGOs, to increase the level of financial literacy of ordinary people. The assumption was that, if people are financially literate, they will not make wrong investment/ consumption decisions and they will not be easily deceived by "improper offers", individually and collectively. Although some financial literacy of people may be good, this approach cannot even get close to achieving the desired goal of disciplining the industry. What the world needs is not a population good at counting money, but properly educated financial professionals to properly manage other people's money. A society is better and more productive when financial professionals are truly trustworthy and talented people but make up only a very tiny portion of the population. Unfortunately, we are far from there.

There is an urgent need for an overall revision of finance (and economics) education at universities. A good start will be to accept that financial theory is based on an untestable assumption of rational investors maximizing a proverbial utility function and its validity could never be proven empirically. For instance, all of the linear pricing models including the celebrated Capital Asset Pricing Model (CAPM) and all factor-investing models are mechanically based on the landmark portfolio theory of Harry Markowitz (1952). The theory applies convex optimization to asset allocation and computes a set of optimal portfolios, which have the minimum possible risk for a given level of return. However, it has been shown repeatedly that *optimal* portfolios perform worse than *naive* portfolios of equal investment in each asset. Ignoring risks gives better results than taking them into consideration. Portfolio theory is only one example. The theory of finance is conceptually flawed and its disconnect from reality has been more obvious since the late 1990s. Financialization has invalidated the very models it feeds on. But we continue to teach them without much questioning. Then the question is: how ethical is it to teach a theory which is known to be wrong?

In addition to their questionable assumptions about human behavior, economic and financial theory are based on a misjudged use of mathematics and even then on a tiny subset of mathematics; calculus and probability theory. Any experienced mathematician with some knowledge of the complexity of finance can infer that calculus and probability alone are grossly inadequate to describe the financial markets of today. These tools can be used to take snapshots of economic problems but not to predict them. The economics profession is good at defining problems but not at solving them. Topics of mathematics used in economics are more from physics than from biology. This has resulted in a focus on defining a unique equilibrium in markets, and neglects the dynamic story of how quickly investor attitudes and behavior change with events. Remember Lucas' (2009) reply to Queen Elizabeth's question about the 2008 crisis: "economic theory has established that it cannot predict such crises". Indeed it cannot. We must free economics from this deadlock.

Internet-based platforms such as Google and Amazon heavily use tools of data science to watch the economy in order to develop and update their business models. Apparently, it has proven very helpful for them. Tools of big data technologies such as artificial intelligence and machine learning have also penetrated the financial industry for such purposes as understanding customer behavior with credit cards and also for more complex cases such as global asset management. In recent years, computer scientists with expertise in big data have been replacing economists with expertise in calculus, and for good reason.

Information technology can help modernize finance and economics curricula. In addition to basic knowledge on artificial intelligence and machine learning, we have to teach new areas of mathematics such as complexity theory, experimental mathematics and even models of biological evolution. Equipped with such capabilities, economists will be freed from having to make unrealistic assumptions about investor behavior to develop evolutionary models of multiple equilibria. If this cannot be done, then the intellectual capture of the industry by the now old-fashioned economists will end, and we will see the "Big Brother" capturing the industry's mindset. This will be the end of consumer protection as we know it. Bad finance has been harmful enough and we do not want our societies to face worse finance further empowered by technology. Universities must update their programs on finance and economics now.

Last but not least, we should first teach students why finance exists in societies, its purposes and functions, and how they are expected to serve the society at large. This necessarily touches on issues of morality, ethics and a culture of sharing. We have to teach that finance professionals are entrusted with management of other people's money. They are expected to maximize the interest of their customers without jeopardizing their companies, and *not* to maximize the interest of their companies without jeopardizing the interest of customers. Trading with customer's money is acceptable as long as its returns and risks are fairly and transparently shared with the customer. These must be the criteria in innovating new products and in seeking regulatory clearance. Prudence and compliance are important but integrity is more important. In all paths of life, a wise person is one who first seeks an answer to "Why?" before finding out "How?" Such wise behavior is also an integral part of financial ethics because finance is all about trusted intermediation. This is the career they must be prepared for.

FOUR

Final Words

Finance is one of the most vital infrastructures of modern societies. Social and economic welfare depend on the quality of financial services. In free and democratic societies, scientific advances cannot be transformed into goods and services without properly allocated and utilized capital. Much like blood circulation in the human body, finance has to be invisible externally but smoothly flowing internally. Finance has to be the problem solver but not the problem maker. The pages of the *Financial Times* or *Wall Street Journal* should not be occupied by gloomy news every day.

Unfortunately, the world today is nowhere close to this description of finance. Finance has turned into more of a trouble maker than a service industry. Financial intermediation has become an end in itself. There are fundamental problems in the financial system and flaws in our knowledge of finance. Starting with a major reform in financial education, we must reset our minds and act fast to cure finance. Or we may soon run the risk of an unpredictable disruption in the world order.

Problem areas were explained and possible solutions were proposed. In one sentence, the financial industry has evolved into a self-serving complex system sustainable only through a continually increasing supply of credit. As such, it has become more harmful than useful for the society. Businessmen with entrepreneurial ambitions try hard to stay away from the finance industry as much as they can. The 2008 financial crisis left a populace distrustful of financial firms and public authorities.

As explained with several examples in the book, the first step towards good finance is to break the growing vicious cycle of credit and debt. Short of this, regulation can never save the system, and it will always have to save the firms at the expense of the people. In a properly regulated industry, fates of firms are determined in free markets, not by governments. A functional approach to regulation is much needed.

Like two parties who disagree cannot agree on what they disagree about, we cannot design a model of good finance without redefining the basic reasons why finance exists as a discipline and practice. We must show the courage to question the existing assumptions and set of tools of finance and economics. This book hopes to be a first step to this end.

Notes

1   A crisis is said to happen if one or more of four events take place on a rolling one-year basis: (1) stock market drops 15% or more; (2) exchange rate versus USD drops by 10% or more; (3) government bonds return −10% or less; or (4) sovereign debt defaults during the year.

2   Based on less restrictive criteria, the IMF counts more than 396 banking and currency crises between 1980 and 2012.

3   Technically, in equilibrium, the properly discounted present value of financial assets must be equal to that of real assets, considering various risks assumed by holders of financial claims.

4   Advanced economies are Australia, Austria, Belgium, Canada, Denmark, Estonia, Finland, France, Germany, Greece, Italy, Japan, Latvia, Lithuania, Norway, Portugal, Slovak Republic, Slovenia, Spain, Sweden, Switzerland, United Kingdom, and United States. Emerging economies are Argentina, Brazil, Chile, China, Colombia, Czech Republic, Hungary, India, Indonesia, Korea, Malaysia, Mexico, Peru, Philippines, Poland, Russia, Saudi Arabia, South Africa, Thailand and Turkey. This grouping is used here for comparability with other studies.

5   As an interesting case, in 2018, the global cross-border money transfers between businesses is estimated to total $155 trillion, against a total trade volume of say $50 trillion plus a few trillions of FDI flows.

6   With Brexit prospects so real these days, the economic and social consequences of London losing its stardom as a financial center may have to be thought through carefully.

7 These numbers do not include capital gains on proprietory trading of securities by investment banks and hence they may be understatements to some extent.

8 It may be noted that 8% of $19 trillion of US GDP and 5% of $30 trillion of (non-US) OECD GDP in 2017 adds up to a total income of about $3 trillion to owners and employees of financial institutions.

9 See Reinhart and Rogoff (2010); Cecchetti et al (2011); Cournède et al (2015); Gertler (2015); Mian and Sufi (2015); Benczúr et al (2017); Lane and Milesi-Ferretti (2017).

10 As a rare case for comfort, it is good to see high talent also going into technology sectors in recent years.

11 Relatively, the smallest decrease is seen in the UK but this may be a little misleading. The London Stock Exchange has three markets: Main Market, Alternative Investments Market (AIM) and Professional Securities Market (PSM). The number of domestic public companies in the Main Market, where most of the market value lies, has significantly declined but this decline has been partially offset by increases in AIM for smaller companies, in PSM for international companies and also recent listings of foreign companies in the Main Market.

12 Eventually, Exxon had to pay about $3.8 billion in environmental and personal damages related to the spill.

13 Vivango is basically a straight bond with a variable rate of interest equal to 70% of the payoff on an Asian-type call option written on sequentially better performing stocks in the Eurostoxx 50 index. Understood?

14 As these firms may also cross-invest, there may be a slight double counting in the total sum.

15 In a survey of 401 Chief Financial Officers (CFOs) of US companies, Graham and colleagues (2005, 67) found that they would "give up positive NPV projects to meet short-term earnings benchmarks…" The study concluded: "In the end, many of our results are disturbing. A majority of these CFO's admit they would sacrifice long-term economic value to hit a target or to smooth short-term earnings".

16 A letter from the Committee on Oversight and Government Reform of the US Congress to the SEC in 2011, asking why small companies cannot access public markets, is full of lessons for all today.

17 Moving in the opposite direction, Karl Marx denied any merit in free markets and instead focused on the social impacts of capital. Marx's ideas triggered communist revolutions all over the world for more than a century and ended as a colossal economic failure with the collapse of the Soviet Union.

18 It is interesting to note that, despite his description of free markets as casinos, Keynes is claimed to have made a fortune on the stock market. People do not make fortunes by gambling.

19 In simple terms, a market is "complete" when all assets can be priced in all states of the world. This is possible when there are no market imperfections such as transaction costs and asymmetric regulation. The concept is the cornerstone of modern financial theory.

20 A joint conference by the Hutchins Center at the Brookings Institution and the Yale Program on Financial Stability, hosted by Andrew Sorkin of the *New York Times* and CNBC, on September 18, 2018. The video is available at www.brookings.edu/events/day-2-responding-to-the-global-financial-crisis/

21 Margaret Atwood's book *Payback* is an enjoyable read about the concept of debt in human history.

22 In light of recent debates about cryptocurrencies like Bitcoin, it may be provocative to note that more than 90% of "money" is actually "digital money", stored as digital records in banks' computers.

Bibliography

Note on data sources

Unless otherwise specifically stated below the figures, the raw data behind all figures in the book are obtained from various public sources and they are either used directly or combined and consolidated by the author. The data can be obtained by querying and downloading the desired variables via the following URLs:

[1] Bank for International Settlements (BIS): www.bis.org/statistics
[2] International Monetary Fund (IMF): www.imf.org/external/ datamapper/datasets/GDD; www.imf.org/en/Research/ commodity-prices and https://data.imf.org
[3] Organization for Economic Co-operation and Development (OECD): https://stats.oecd.org; www.oecd.org/finance/oecd-business-and-finance-scoreboard.htm
[4] Philippon, T. http://pages.stern.nyu.edu/~tphilipp/research.htm (click Data Series)
[5] Shiller, R. www.econ.yale.edu/~shiller/data/Fig3-1.xls
[6] World Bank: https://databank.worldbank.org/data/source/world-development-indicators
[7] World Federation of Exchanges (WFE): www.world-exchanges. org/our-work/statistics

Admati, A.R. and M. Hellwig (2013) *The Bankers' New Clothes: What is Wrong with Banking and What to Do about It*, Princeton: Princeton University Press.

Adrian, T. and B. Jones (2018) "Shadow Banking and Market-Based Finance", IMF, Monetary and Capital Markets Department report 18/14.

Aldasoro, I. and T. Ehlers (2018) "The Credit Default Swap Market: What a Difference a Decade Makes", *BIS Quarterly Review*, June: 1–4.

Amberber, E. (2015) "'Banking is necessary, banks are not' – 7 quotes from Bill Gates on mobile banking", *YourStory*, January 22, https//yourstory.com/2015/01/quotes-bill-gates-mobile-banking

Antill, S., D. Hou and A. Sarkar (2014) "The Growth of Murky Finance", *Liberty Street Economics*, https://libertystreeteconomics.newyorkfed.org/2014/03/

Arrow, K.J. (1963) *Social Choice and Individual Values*, New Haven: Yale University Press.

Atwood, M. (2008) *Payback: Debt and the Dark Side of Wealth*, Toronto: Anansi Press.

Bachelier, L. (1900) *Théorie de la Spéculation*, Paris: Gauthier Villars.

Bank for International Settlements (2017) *87th Annual Report*, Basel, www.bis.org

Barth, J.R., G. Caprio Jr. and R. Levine (2012) *Guardians of Finance*, Cambridge, MA: The MIT Press.

Benczúr, P., S. Karagiannis and V. Kvedaras (2017) "Finance and Economic Growth", Working paper 2017/7, *Joint Research Centre*, the European Commission.

Black, F. and M. Scholes (1973) "The Pricing of Options and Corporate Liabilities", *Journal of Political Economy*, 81(3): 637–654.

Blanchard, O., D. Romer, M. Spence and J. Stiglitz, eds (2017) *In the Wake of the Crisis*, Cambridge, MA: The MIT Press.

Bookstaber, R. (2017) *The End of Theory*, Princeton: Princeton University Press.

Buffett, W. (2002) *Chairman's Letter to the Shareholders of Berkshire Hathaway Inc*, www.berkshirehathaway.com/letters/2002pdf.pdf

Cecchetti, S.G. and E. Kharroubi (2015) "Why Does Financial Sector Growth Crowd Out Real Economic Growth", *BIS Working Papers*, No 490.

Cecchetti, S.G., M.S. Mohanty and F. Zampolli (2011) "The Real Effects of Debt", *BIS Working Papers*, No 352.

Célérier, C. and B. Vallée (2014) "What Drives Financial Complexity? A Look into the Retail Market for Structured Products", www.semanticscholar.org/

Çelik, S. and M. Isaksson (2017) "Adapting Global Standards to a Changing World", *10th Year Anniversary Essay*, Millstein Center, Columbia University.

Chambers, D. and E. Dimson, eds (2016) *Financial Market History*, Charlottesville, VA: The CFA Institute Research Foundation.

Cournède, B. and O. Denk (2015a) "Finance and Economic Growth in OECD and G20 Countries", Economics Department Working Papers 1223, OECD.

Cournède, B. and O. Denk (2015b) "Finance and Income Inequality in OECD Countries", Economics Department Working Papers 1224, OECD.

Cournède, B., O. Denk and P. Hoeller (2015) "Finance and Inclusive Growth", Economic Policy Paper 14, OECD.

Cunningham, L.A. (2013) *The Essays of Warren Buffett*, Durham: Carolina Associated Press.

Dalio, R. (2018) *A Template for Understanding Big Debt Crises*, Westport, CT: Bridgewater Associates.

Debreu, G. (1959) *Theory of Value*, New Haven: Yale University Press.

Desai, M.A. (2017) *The Wisdom of Finance*, Boston: Houghton Mifflin Harcourt.

Di Noia, C. (2018) "The EU Securities Law Framework for SMEs: Can Firms and Investors Meet?", in C. Mayer et al (eds), *Finance and Investment: The European Case*, Oxford: Oxford University Press.

Dimson, E., P. Marsh and M. Staunton (2002) *Triumph of the Optimists: 101 Years of Global Investment Returns*, Princeton: Princeton University Press.

Dimson, E., P. Marsh and M. Staunton (2017) *The 2017 Global Investment Returns Yearbook*, Zurich: Credit Suisse Research Institute.

Dudley, W.C. (2017) "Lessons from the Financial Crisis", Remarks at the Economic Club of New York, www.bis.org/review/r171107b. htm

El-Arian, M.A. (2016) *The Only Game in Town*, New York: Random House.

Fama, E.F. (1970) "Efficient Capital Markets: A Review of Theory and Empirical Work", *Journal of Finance*, 25(2): 383–417.

Forbes Magazine (2018) *The World's Billionaires 2018*, www.forbes. com/billionaires/list/

Francis, J. (1850) "Chronicles and Characters of the Stock Exchange", *The Church of England Quarterly Review*, 27(6): 128-155.

Friedman, M. (1969) *The Optimum Quantity of Money and Other Essays*, Chicago: Aldine.

Galbraith, J.K. (1993) *A Short History of Financial Euphoria*, New York: Penguin Books.

Gertler, M. (2015) "What Happened: Financial Factors in the Great Recession", NBER Working Paper, www.nber.org/papers/ w24746

Global Financial Stability Report (2018) "A Bumpy Road Ahead", www.imf.org/publications/gfsr

Goetzman, W.N. and K.G. Rouwenhorst (2005) *The Origins of Values*, Oxford: Oxford University Press.

Graeber, D. (2012) *Debt: The First 5,000 Years*, London: Melville House Publishing.

Graham, J.R., C.R. Harvey and S. Rajgopal (2005) "The Economic Implications of Corporate Financial Reporting", *Journal of Accounting and Economics*, 40: 3-73.

Greenspan, A. (2011) "Dodd-Frank Fails to Meet Test of our Times", *Financial Times*, March 29.

Greenwood, R. and D. Scharfstein (2013) "The Growth of Finance", *Journal of Economic Perspectives*, 27(2): 3-28.

Guillen, M.F. (2012) "The Global Economic & Financial Crisis: A Timeline", The Lauder Institute, University of Pennsylvania.

Haldane, A. (2010) "Patience and Finance", speech at the Oxford China Business Forum, Beijing, www.bis.org/review/r100909e.pdf

Haldane, A. (2014) "Managing Global Finance as a System", Speech at Maxwell Fry Annual Global Finance Lecture, Birmingham University, October 29.

Harari, Y.N. (2018) Money, London: Vintage Minis.

Hawksworth, J., R. Clary and H. Audino (2017) "The Long View: How Will the Global Economic Order Change by 2050?", London: PricewaterhouseCoopers.

Hicks, J. (1937) "Mr. Keynes and the 'Classics': A Suggested Interpretation", Econometrica, 5: 147-159.

Issa, D., Chairman (2011) Letter from the "Committee on Oversight and Government Reform" of the US Congress to M.L. Schapiro, Chairman of the Securities and Exchange Commission, March 22, www.slideshare.net.

Jevons, W.S. (1879/2008) The Theory of Political Economy, Whitefish: Kessinger Publishing.

Kay, J. (2015) Other People's Money, London: Profile Books.

Keynes, J.M. (1936) The General Theory of Employment, Interest and Money, London: Macmillan.

Krugman, P. (2009) "How Did Economists Get It So Wrong?", The New York Times Magazine, www.nytimes.com/2009/09/06/magazine/06Economic-t.html

Lane, P.R. and G.M. Milesi-Ferretti (2017) "International Financial Integration in the Aftermath of the Global Financial Crisis", IMF Working Paper 17/115.

Lewis, M. (2008) "Bear Stearns Proves Bank CEOs Don't Have a Clue About Credit Crunch Crisis", Evening Standard, March 27.

Lowenstein, R. (2000) When Genius Failed: The Rise and Fall of LTCM, New York: Random House.

Lucas, R. (2003) "Macroeconomic Priorities," American Economic Review, 93(1): 1-4.

Lucas, R. (2009) "In Defense of the Dismal Science", *The Economist*, August 6, www.economist.com/node/14165405

Lund, S., J. Woetzel, E. Windhagen, R. Dobbs and D. Goldshtein (2018) "Rising Corporate Debt: Peril or Promise?", Discussion Paper, McKinsey Global Institute.

Mandelbrot, B. (1963) "The Variation of Certain Speculative Prices", *Journal of Business*, 36: 392-417.

Markowitz, H. (1952) "Portfolio Selection", *Journal of Finance*, 7(1): 77-91.

Merton, R.C. (1973) "The Theory of Rational Option Pricing", *Bell Journal of Economics and Management Science*, 4(1): 141-183.

Mian, A. and A. Sufi (2015) *House of Debt*, Chicago: The University of Chicago Press.

Mian, A. and A. Sufi (2018) "Credit Supply and Housing Speculation", NBER Working Paper: 24823.

Mill, J.S. (1848) *Principles of Political Economy*, London: J.W. Parker.

Millstein, I.M. (2017) *The Activist Director*, New York: Columbia University Press.

Minsky, H.P. (1982) *Can "It" Happen Again? Essays on Instability and Finance*, New York: M.E. Sharpe.

Modigliani, F. and M.H. Miller (1958) "The Cost of Capital, Corporation Finance, and the Theory of Investment", *American Economic Review*, 48(3): 261-297.

Muscatov, A. and M. Peres (2016) "Shadow Banking Reemerges, Posing Challenges to Banks and Regulators", *Economic Letter*, Federal Reserve Bank of Dallas, www.dallasfed.org/~/media/documents/research/eclett/2016/el1610.pdf

OECD (2012) "Debt and Macroeconomic Stability", OECD Economics Department Policy Notes, 16.

Philippon, T. (2015) "Has the US Finance Industry Become Less Efficient? On the Theory and Measurement of Financial Intermediation", *American Economic Review*, 105(4): 1408-38.

Plender, J. (2016) *Capitalism: Money, Morals and Markets*, London: Biteback Publishing.

Reid, J., C. Nicol, N. Burns and S. Chanda (2017) "Long-Term Asset Return Study: The Next Financial Crisis", London: Deutsche Bank AG.

Reinhart, C.M. and K.S. Rogoff (2009) *This Time Is Different: Eight Centuries of Financial Folly,* Princeton: Princeton University Press.

Reinhart, C.M. and K.S. Rogoff (2010) "Growth in a Time of Debt", *American Economic Review,* 100(2): 573-578.

Ricardo, D. (1817) *On the Principles of Political Economy and Taxation,* London: John Murray.

Rolnick, A. (2012) "Thomas Sargent's Rational Expectations", *Hoover Digest,* www.hoover.org/research/thomas-sargents-rational-expectations

Romer, P. (2016) "The Trouble with Macroeconomics", https://paulromer.net/wp-content/uploads/2016/09/WP-Trouble.pdf

Sahay, R., M. Čihák, P. N'Diaye, A. Barajas, R. Bi, D. Ayala, Y. Gao, A. Kyobe, L. Nguyen, C. Saborowski, K. Svirydzenka and S.R. Yousefi (2015) "Rethinking Financial Deepening: Stability and Growth in Emerging Markets", IMF Staff Discussion Note SDN/15/08.

Samuelson, P.A. (1965) "Proof that Properly Anticipated Prices Fluctuate Randomly", *Industrial Management Review,* 6(2): 41-49.

Schularick, M. (2011) "140 Years of Financial Crises: Old Dog, New Tricks", *Jahrbuch für Wirtschaftsgeschichte,* 1: 45-67.

Schumpeter, J.A. (1934) *The Theory of Economic Development,* Cambridge, MA: Harvard University Press.

Shiller, R.J. (2000) *Irrational Exuberance,* Princeton: Princeton University Press.

Shiller, R.J. (2012) *Finance and the Good Society,* Princeton: Princeton University Press.

Shorrocks, A., J. Davies and R. Lluberas (2018) *Global Wealth Databook 2017,* Zurich: Credit Suisse Research Institute.

Smith, A. (1776) *The Wealth of Nations,* Suffolk: Penguin Books.

Thaler, R.H. (2015) *Misbehaving,* New York: Norton.

The Financial Crisis Inquiry Commission (2011) "The Financial Crisis Inquiry Report", US Government, www.govinfo.gov/app/details/GPO-FCIC

Tirole, J. (2017) *Economics for the Common Good*, Princeton: Princeton University Press.

Tobin, J. (1984) "On the Efficiency of the Financial System", *Lloyds Bank Review*, 153: 1-15.

Tooze, A. (2018) *Crashed: How a Decade of Financial Crises Changed the World*, London: Allen Lane.

Tucker, P. (2018) *Unelected Power: The Quest for Legitimacy in Central Banking and the Regulatory State*, Princeton: Princeton University Press.

Turner, A. (2016) *Between Debt and the Devil*, Princeton: Princeton University Press.

Turner, A., A. Haldane, P. Woolley, S. Wadhwani, C. Goodhart, A. Smithers, A. Large, J. Kay, M. Wolf, P. Boone, S. Johnson and R. Layard (2010) *The Future of Finance: The LSE Report*, London: London School of Economics and Political Science.

Vandevelde, M. (2018) "How the Biggest Private Equity Firms became the New Banks", *Financial Times*, www.ft.com/content/ec43db70-ba8e-11e8-94b2-17176fbf93f5

Wall Street Journal (2009) *Interview* with Paul Volcker, December 14, 2009.

Wikipedia, https://en.wikipedia.org/wiki/South_Sea_Company.

Wilmott, P. (2010) "Viewpoint: The Problem with Derivatives, Quants and Risk-Management Today", in *Qfinance* (3rd ed), London: Bloomsbury, 245-247.

Wolfe, H. (1930) *The Uncelestial City*, London: Gollancz Ltd.

World Trade Organization (2014) "The Rise of Global Value Chains", *World Trade Report 2014*, www.wto.org/english/res_e/booksp_e/wtr14-2c_e.pdf

Zingales, L. (2015) "Presidential Address: Does Finance Benefit Society?", *The Journal of Finance*, 70(4): 1327-1363.

Index